THE ARTIST BEHIND SUPERMAN

THE JOE SHUSTER STORY

STORY

D1333532

This book had many helpers along the way, beginning with my parents, who bought me my first SUPERMAN comic as a kid, to my agent Nicolas Grivel, introducing me to the marvelous artist Thomas Campi. Thomas, thanks for turning my words magically into images. Ray Felix and Arlen Schumer, thank you for your insights and advise, Karen Green thank you for giving me early access to Joe Shuster's letters and Chelle Mayer for sharing family anecdotes.
To Lisa, Leon, and Simon.
—Julian Voloj

I'd like to thank you Julian and Nicolas for this incredible journey that has been making this book.
Thanks to Roberto for the support and advice. Finally thank you to Joe Shuster and Jerry Siegel, not only for creating such an iconic character as Superman, but for reminding me how lucky I am in making comics for a living.
To Elisa and Alex.
—Thomas Campi

Last, but not least, we would like to thank Jim Salicrup and Jeff Whitman for their patient collaboration on this publication, as well as Terry Nantier for believing in this project.
—Julian & Thomas

**THE ARTIST BEHIND SUPERMAN
THE JOE SHUSTER STORY**

THE JOE SHUSTER STORY logo by Thomas Campi and Bryan Senka
Jeff Whitman – Assistant Managing Editor/Production Coordinator
Jim Salicrup
Editor-in-Chief

ISBN: 978-1-62991-777-1 Paperback Edition
ISBN: 978-1-62991-776-4 Hardcover Edition

Super Genius books may be purchased for business or promotional use.
For information on bulk purchases please contact Macmillan Corporate
and Premium Sales Department at (800) 221-7945 x5442.

Distributed by Macmillan.
Super Genius is an imprint of Papercutz.
First Printing
Please visit THE JOE SHUSTER STORY Facebook page:
www.facebook.com/JoeShusterSuperman
www.supergeniuscomics.com

THE ARTIST BEHIND SUPERMAN
THE JOE SHUSTER STORY

JULIAN VOLOJ
WRITER

THOMAS CAMPI
ARTIST

WITH A PREFACE BY
CHELLE MAYER

NEW YORK

GRAPHIC NOVELS AVAILABLE FROM SUPER GENIUS

NEIL GAIMAN'S
LADY JUSTICE
Volume One

NEIL GAIMAN'S
LADY JUSTICE
Volume Two

NEIL GAIMAN'S
TEKNOPHAGE
Volume One

NEIL GAIMAN'S
TEKNOPHAGE
Volume Two

NEIL GAIMAN'S
MR. HERO
Volume One

NEIL GAIMAN'S
MR. HERO
Volume Two

TRISH TRASH #1
Rollergirl of Mars
By Jessica Abel

TRISH TRASH #2
Rollergirl of Mars
By Jessica Abel

THE CHILDREN OF
CAPTAIN GRANT
By Jules Verne
Adapted by Alexis Nesme

THE WENDY
PROJECT
By Melissa Jane Osborne
& Veronica Fish

HIGH MOON #1
David Gallaher &
Steve Ellis

TALES FROM THE CRYPT
By Miran Kim,
Bernie Wrightson,
Jolyon Yates, & others

SUPER GENIUS

Super Genius graphic novels are available at booksellers everywhere. NEIL GAIMAN'S LADY JUSTICE Volume One & Two, NEIL GAIMAN'S TEKNOPHAGE Volume One & Two, and NEIL GAIMAN'S MR. HERO Volume One are $14.99 each in paperback, and $24.99 each in hardcover. THE CHILDREN OF CAPTAIN GRANT is $14.99 in paperback, and $19.99 in hardcover. TRISH TRASH is $14.99 in hardcover only. THE WENDY PROJECT is $12.99 in paperback only. HIGH MOON is $14.99 in paperback, and $24.99 in hardcover. TALES FROM THE CRYPT is $9.99 in paperback, and $14.99 in hardcover. You may also order online at supergeniuscomics.com. Or call 1-800-886-1223, Monday through Friday, 9 – 5 EST. MC, Visa, and AmEx accepted. To order by mail, please add $5.00 for postage and handling for first book ordered, $1.00 for each additional book and make check payable to NBM Publishing. Send to: Super Genius, 160 Broadway, Suite 700, East Wing, New York, NY 10038.

PREFACE

In the 1930s comics were not lucrative or popular as they are today, creating them was not respected, and being Jewish was a valid reason to be denied jobs. Back then, two kids from Cleveland, Jerry Siegel and Joe Shuster, were peddling their Superman story around, which resulted in slammed doors at every turn.

Back then, my grandfather Sheldon "Shelly" Mayer was working for All-Amercan Comics run by Max Gaines at 225 Lafayette Street. When he met them, they had pretty much given up on selling their creation. Jerry and Joe showed their Superman stories to Shelly who knew they were onto something and invited them to his home for dinner.

There the stories were shown to his kid brother Monte, the inspiration for Dinky in Why Big Brothers Leave Home within the Scribbly Comic, who was 10 and often a test case for potential and newly printed comics. The kid loved it, which confirmed Shelly's take.

Back at the office he insisted on the need to print these stories to Max. "They'll be be a hit!" Max had enough titles at that time so he called their uptown office on 45th and Lexington, run by Harry Donenfeld and Jack Leibowitz, who agreed to print Superman.

The rest, is, as they say, history.

I'm excited that Julian Voloj and Thomas Campi are now bringing Superman's origins story in comic book form to the world. Superman is not from Krypton, but from Cleveland, and I'm proud that my grandfather had a hand in introducing him to the world.

–*Chelle Mayer*

Dedicated to Jerry and Joe.

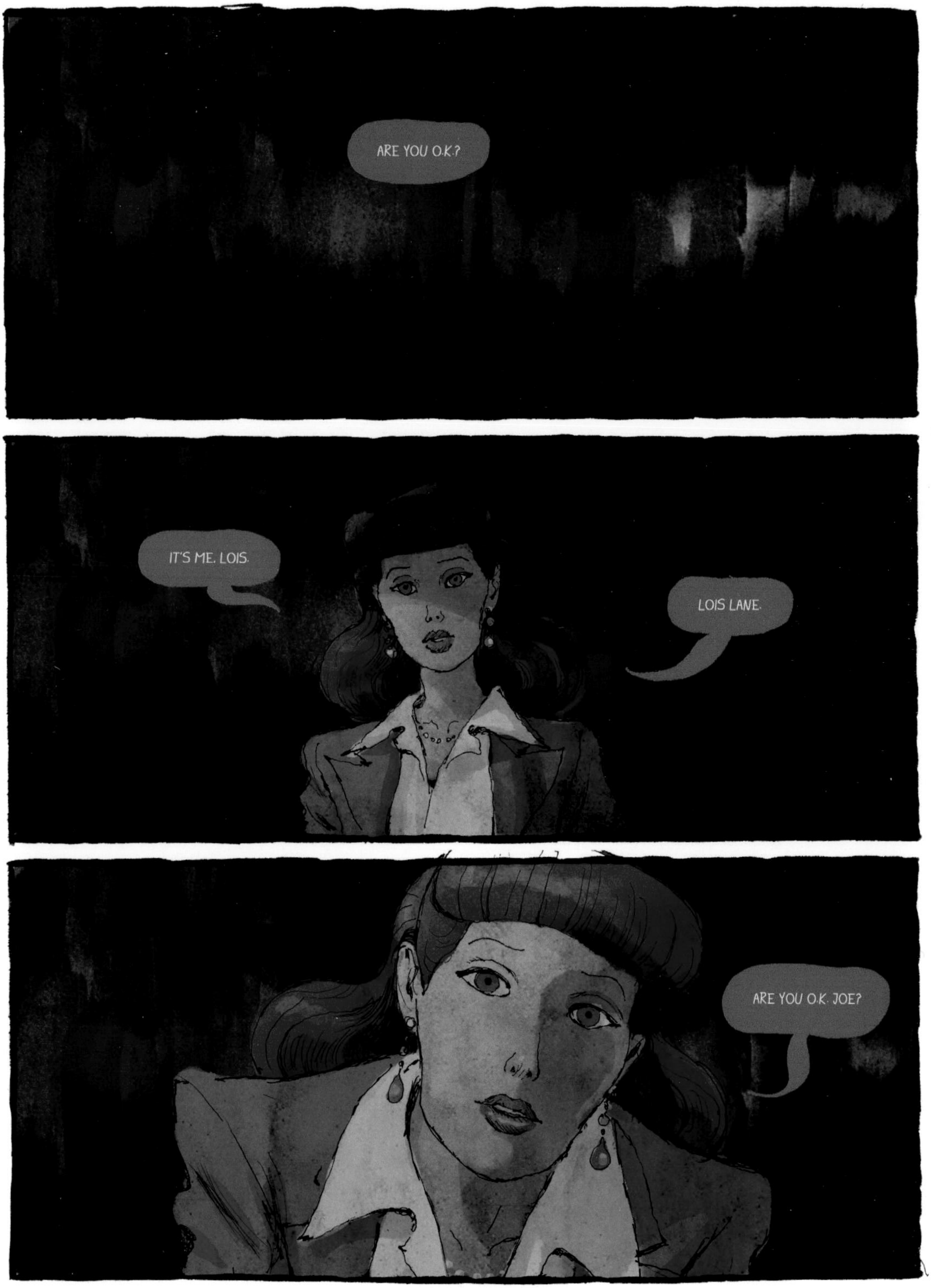
ARE YOU O.K.?
IT'S ME. LOIS.
LOIS LANE.
ARE YOU O.K. JOE?

ARE YOU OK JOE?

IT'S ME, JERRY.
HOW DID YOU BECOME
SO OLD?

I DON'T KNOW. I REALLY DON'T KNOW.

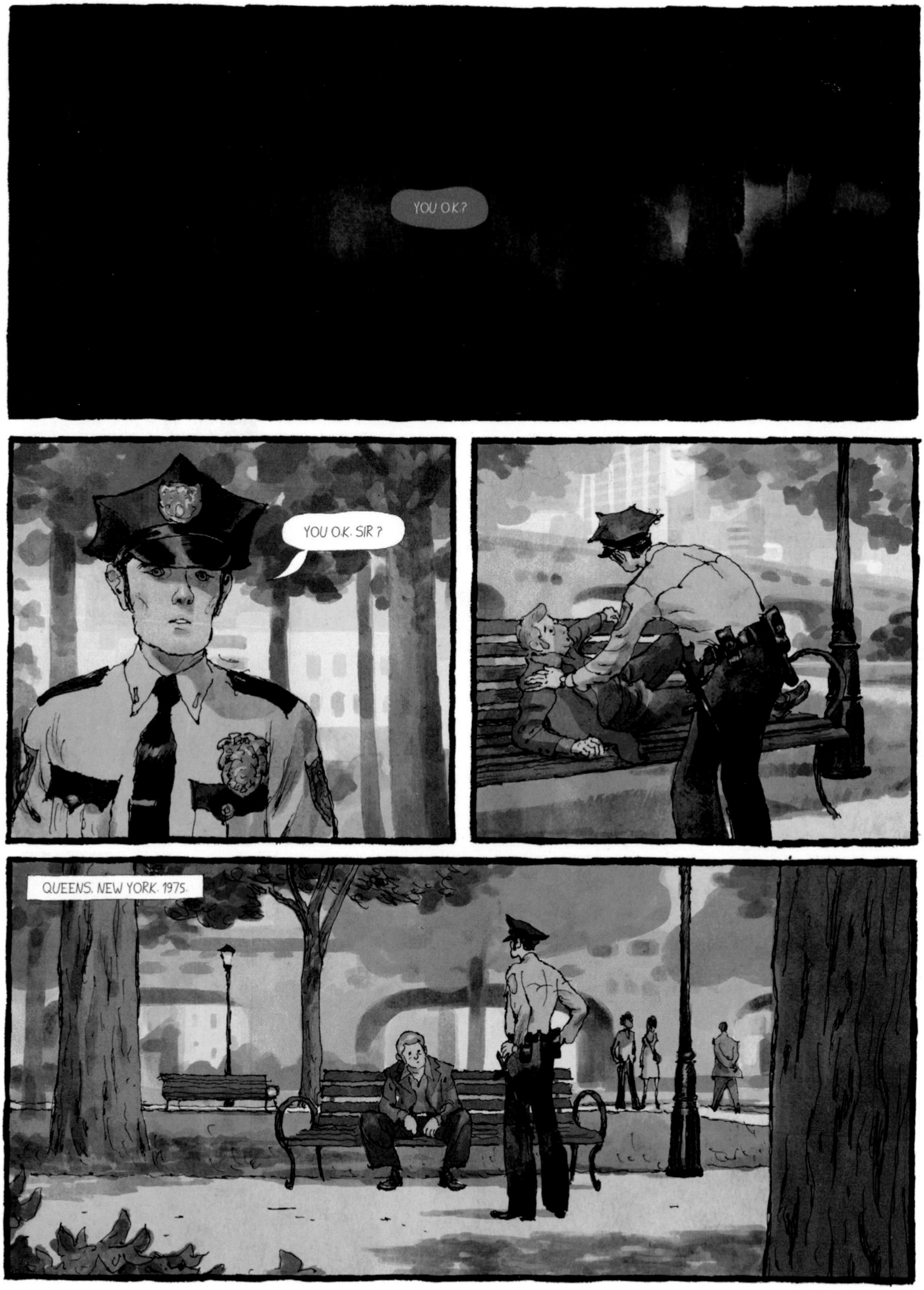
YOU O.K?
YOU O.K. SIR ?
QUEENS, NEW YORK. 1975.

YOU LOOK LIKE YOU HAVEN'T EATEN IN DAYS.

AH...

NO WORRIES. MY TREAT. WHAT D'YOU WANT?

MAYBE SOME SOUP?

SOUP IT IS.

WHAT DIDYA DO FOR A LIVING?

I DID COMICS.

OH. NICE. ANYTHING I WOULD KNOW?

WELL...

DRAW SOMETHING.

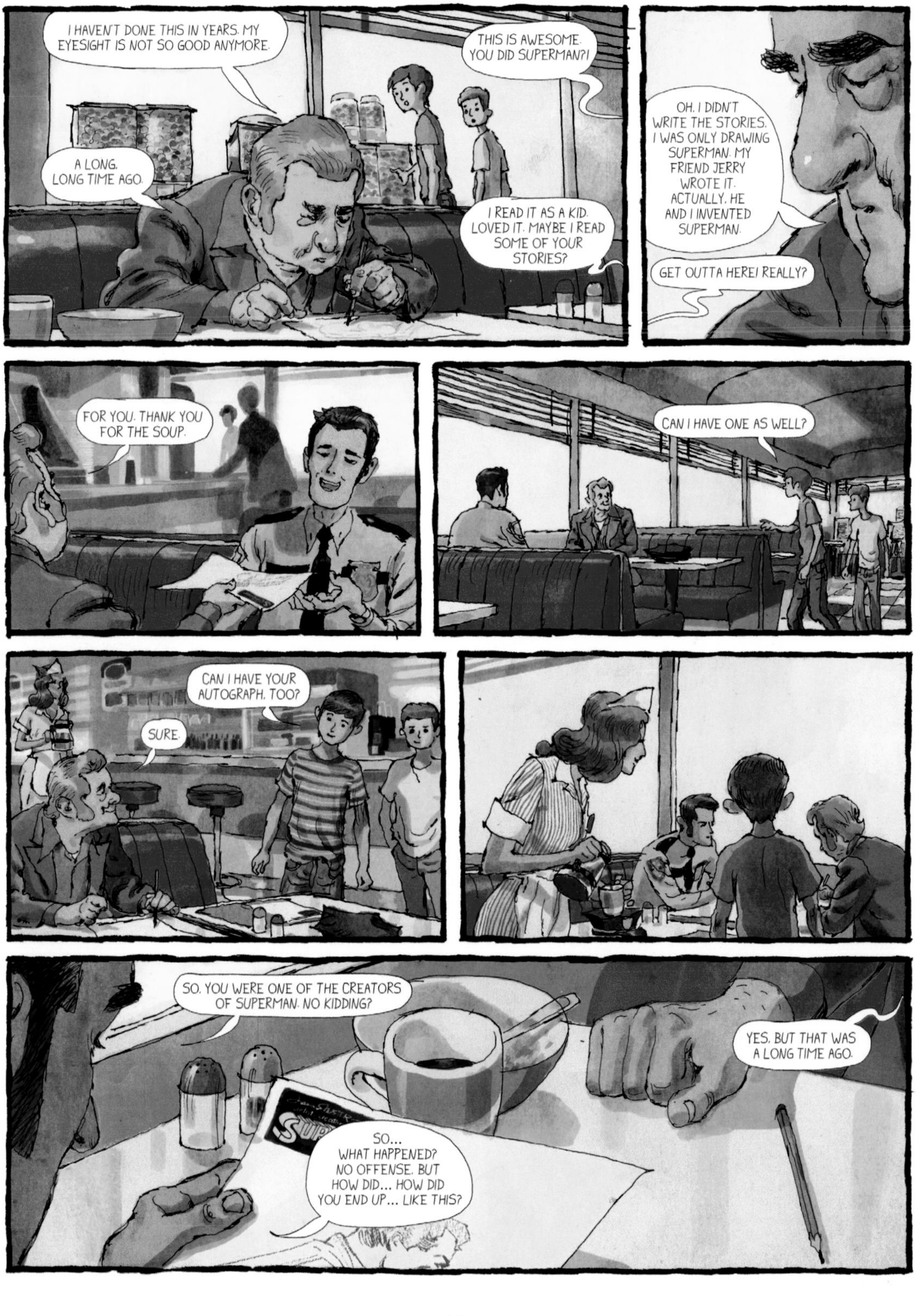
I HAVEN'T DONE THIS IN YEARS. MY EYESIGHT IS NOT SO GOOD ANYMORE.
A LONG, LONG TIME AGO.
THIS IS AWESOME. YOU DID SUPERMAN?!
I READ IT AS A KID. LOVED IT. MAYBE I READ SOME OF YOUR STORIES?
OH, I DIDN'T WRITE THE STORIES. I WAS ONLY DRAWING SUPERMAN. MY FRIEND JERRY WROTE IT. ACTUALLY, HE AND I INVENTED SUPERMAN.
GET OUTTA HERE! REALLY?
FOR YOU. THANK YOU FOR THE SOUP.
CAN I HAVE ONE AS WELL?
CAN I HAVE YOUR AUTOGRAPH, TOO?
SURE.
SO, YOU WERE ONE OF THE CREATORS OF SUPERMAN. NO KIDDING?
YES, BUT THAT WAS A LONG TIME AGO.
SO... WHAT HAPPENED? NO OFFENSE, BUT HOW DID... HOW DID YOU END UP... LIKE THIS?

I never met my grandparents. They were all from Russia, from some of these places in the middle of nowhere that changed names and borders all the time.

My mother did not speak much about the Old World. I only know she was from Russia, the country that infamously invented the word 'pogrom.'

At some point, she and her sister decided that they had enough of pogroms and poverty and left.

In Rotterdam, they stayed at a hotel run by a Russian Jewish couple who had come there in the hope of moving to America, but ended up staying.

That's how my mom and her sister met my father and my uncle.

They had one week before their passage to Canada, and during that week fell in love with the owners' sons.

They all got married and ended up moving together to Toronto.

Two years after their arrival in Canada, and ten months after my parents got married, I was born in Toronto.

We moved a lot when I was a kid. We lived on Bathurst Street, then on Oxford Street, and after that on Borden Street.

Money was tight, and when rent became a problem we had to move.

At some point, to cut expenses, we shared a house with my uncle and aunt's family.

Their oldest son, Frank, was two years younger and we became close friends. Frank and his family lived downstairs, and we lived upstairs.

Frank's father, my Uncle Jack, worked as a projectionist in a cinema. He would take us to the projector room and we would watch movies together.

We became ardent movie-goers, often spending an entire day together watching silent pictures in the downtown theater where Uncle Jack worked.

Even years later, after I moved to Cleveland and only visited for the summer...

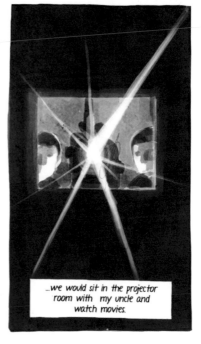

...we would sit in the projector room with my uncle and watch movies.

I liked the movies, but I loved the funnies. That's what they called the comics back then.

During the week, the strips were black and white, but on weekends they were printed in bright, vivid colors.

In those days, they devoted an entire page to one comic.

I was maybe three or four years old and couldn't read yet. So Father and I had a ritual.

We would both open up the color comics and my father would read them to me.

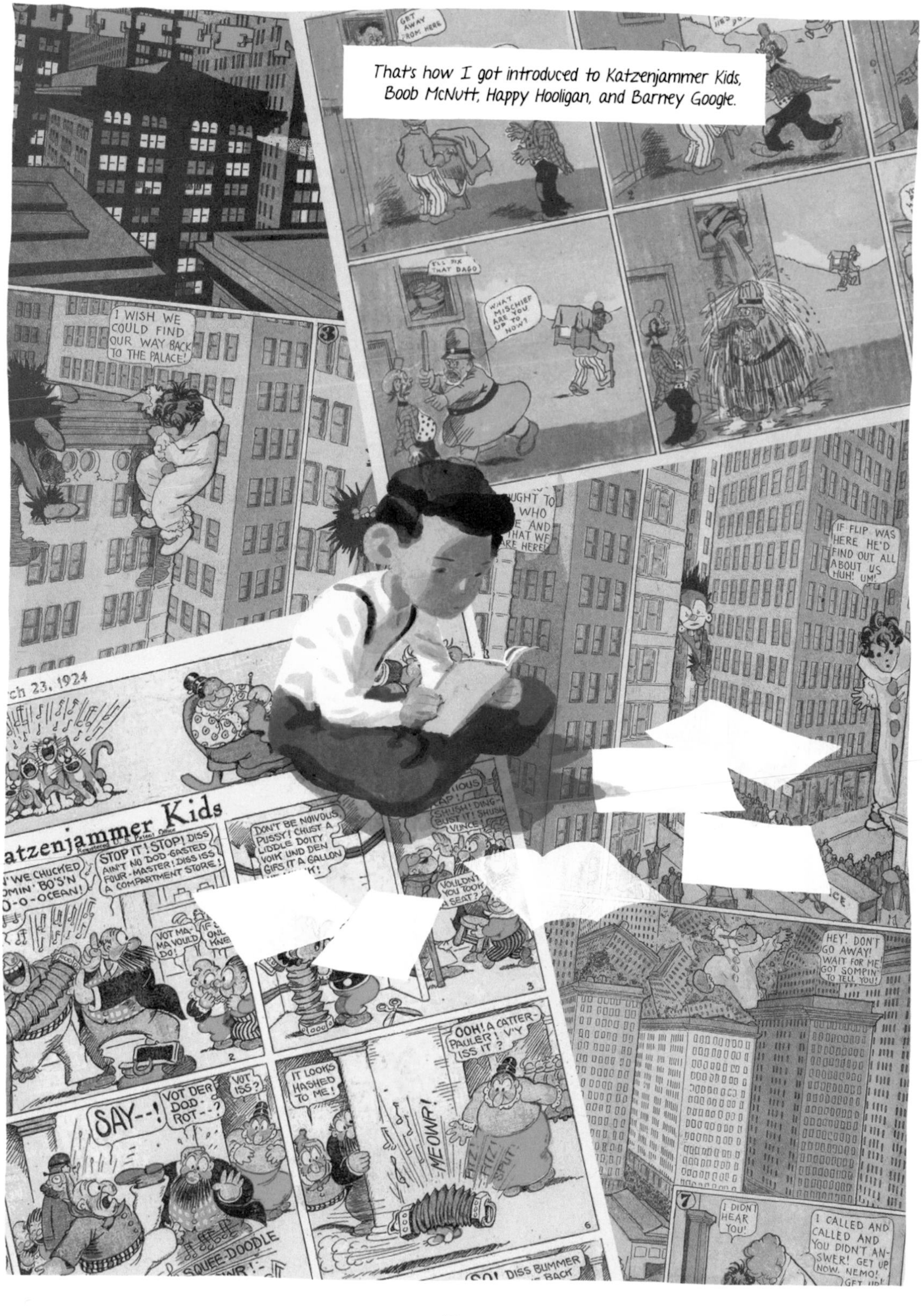
That's how I got introduced to Katzenjammer Kids, Boob McNutt, Happy Hooligan, and Barney Google.
I WISH WE COULD FIND OUR WAY BACK TO THE PALACE!
WHAT MISCHIEF ARE YOU UP TO NOW?
IF FLIP WAS HERE HE'D FIND OUT ALL ABOUT US HUH! UM!
Katzenjammer Kids
STOP IT! STOP! DISS AIN'T NO DOD-GASTED FOUR-MASTER! DISS ISS A COMPARTMENT STORE!
DON'T BE NOIVOUS PUSSY! CHUST A LIDDLE DOITY VOIK UND DEN GIFS IT A GALLON
VOULDN'T YOU TOOK A SEAT?
HEY! DON'T GO AWAY! WAIT FOR ME! GOT SOMPIN' TO TELL YOU!
OOH! A CATTER-PAULER? V'Y ISS IT?
IT LOOKS HASHED TO ME!
SAY--!
VOT DER DOD ROT--?
VOT ISS?
MEOWR!
SQUEE-DOODLE
I DIDN'T HEAR YOU!
I CALLED AND CALLED AND YOU DIDN'T ANSWER! GET UP NOW, NEMO!

SHUSTERLAND

My absolute favorite: Little Nemo in Slumberland. It was a very imaginative strip, and it even had a touch of science fiction in it.

It had marvelous scenes, Winsor McCay's depiction of the city of the future, the planets... all the things I loved.

Later on, I began to read the comics myself, and I had hopes of someday drawing a comic strip of my own.

He gave people credit, even though he knew they would never pay him. My father was a good-hearted man, and people took advantage of him.

Even if our family name ("Shuster") meant 'shoemaker,' my father was a tailor. From what I heard, an excellent one, but unfortunately a very bad businessman. He charged too little, then took too long to stitch.

When I was about ten years old, he learned about a job opportunity at Richman Brothers, so we moved to Cleveland, Ohio.

We took the train. Such an adventure!

Back then, Cleveland had the third largest population in the U.S. after New York and Chicago, and it was the railroad link between them.

The Ohio Bell Building became the city's first skyscraper.

Shortly afterwards the Terminal Tower opened.

We lived southeast of Downtown.

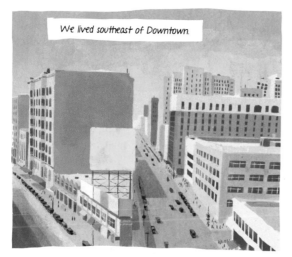

I attended Alexander Hamilton Junior High. It was a brand new school and you could still smell the fresh paint on the walls.

Thinking of it, maybe that's why I wanted to become an illustrator. My mother wanted me to become a doctor, of course. Every Jewish mother's dream.

May I help you?

Ahm, me?

Yes. Is there anyone else standing at the door?

The school had a newspaper called 'The Federalist.'

I was wondering...

Yes?

I would like to help... with the paper.

What can you do?

I draw.

O.K., so bring us something by Friday and then we'll see.

O.K.

Anything else?

What should I bring?

Well, you come up with something.

O.K.

A week later...

It was my first publication. Nothing great. Just one single panel. But it was my first artwork in print. I was so proud.

I did a few more things for the paper.

Nice try.

That's where I met Jerry.

I'm Jerry Fine.

Joe Shuster. Nice to meet you.

Jerry was a reporter for The Federalist. We immediately became friends.

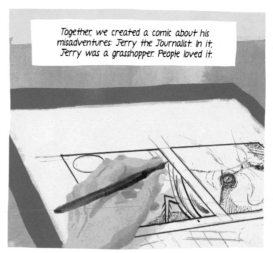

Together, we created a comic about his misadventures: Jerry the Journalist. In it, Jerry was a grasshopper. People loved it.

Life was good.

But then my father lost his job at Richman.

We had to move. Again.

I'm transferring to Glenville High.

My cousin goes to Glenville High. You should look him up I think you guys would like each other. His name's Jerry, too. Jerry Siegel.

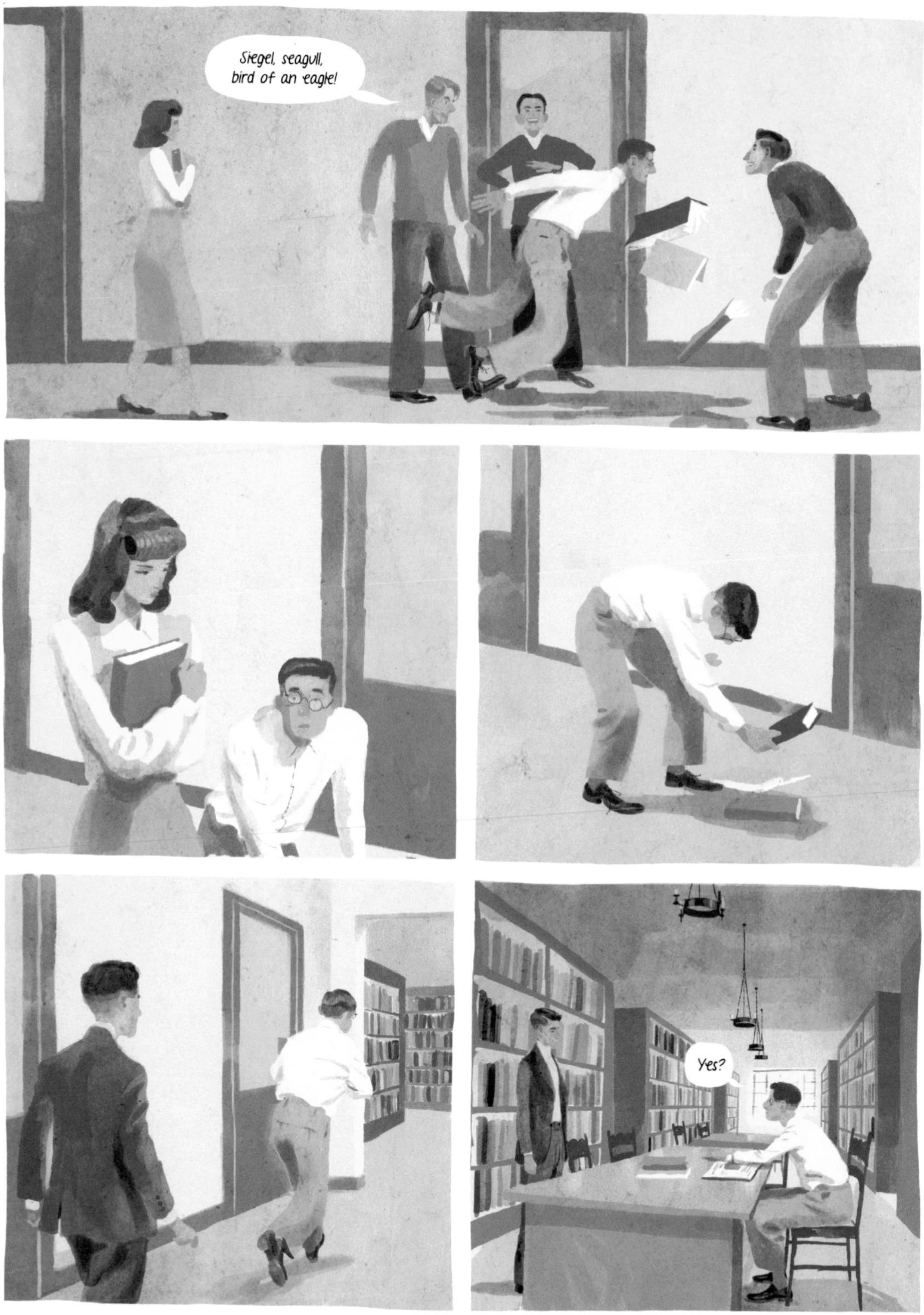
Siegel, seagull, bird of an eagle!
Yes?

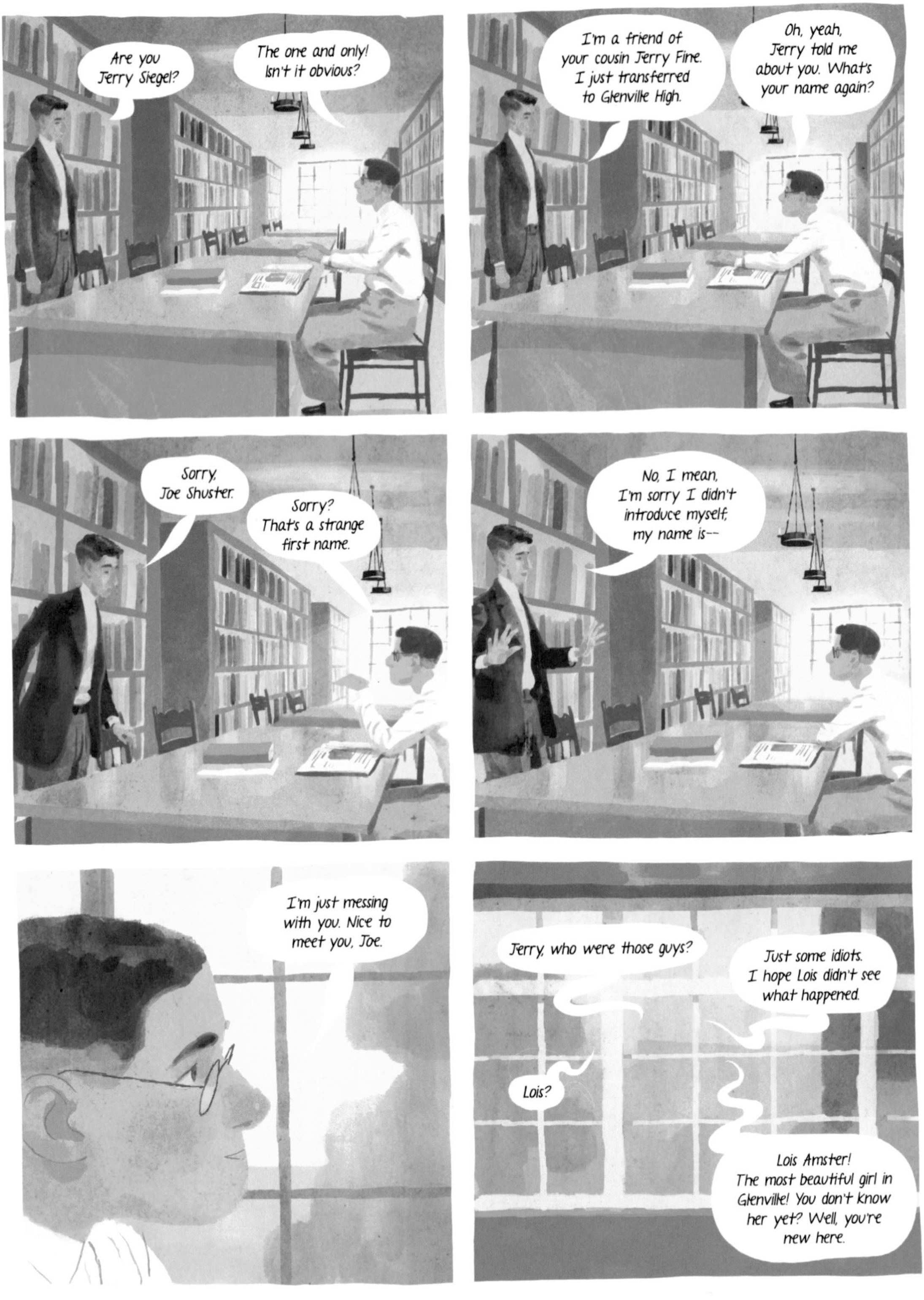
Are you Jerry Siegel?
The one and only! Isn't it obvious?
I'm a friend of your cousin Jerry Fine. I just transferred to Glenville High.
Oh, yeah, Jerry told me about you. What's your name again?
Sorry, Joe Shuster.
Sorry? That's a strange first name.
No, I mean, I'm sorry I didn't introduce myself, my name is--
I'm just messing with you. Nice to meet you, Joe.
Jerry, who were those guys?
Just some idiots. I hope Lois didn't see what happened.
Lois?
Lois Amster! The most beautiful girl in Glenville! You don't know her yet? Well, you're new here.

Have you read 'Ralph 124 C 41+'?

Have I read it?! Excuse me, Mr. Shuster, do you know who you are talking to? Jerry Siegel, scholar of science fiction and popular culture! Of course, I read it. Gernsback's a genius! The title alone, using numbers...

...as a code for the message 'one to foresee for one another.'

Jerry and I hit it off immediately.

His parents were from Lithuania and he was the youngest of six children. Like my dad, his father was a tailor, but apparently a slightly better businessman. He had his own clothing store and they had a nice house on Kimberly, just a few blocks north of us.

This is 'Tarzan of the Apes' by Edgar Rice Burroughs.

They even had a radio in their house.

We first lived on Morison, and then we moved a block north to Armor Avenue, where rent was cheaper.

Eventually my father found work as an elevator operator at Mount Sinai Hospital.

Every job has its ups and downs.

Now watch out!

Jerome Siegel! What are you doing?

I'm flying.

How old are you?!

Bye, Mrs. Siegel.

On Wednesdays, when all the magazines came out, Jerry and I would go to St. Clair Avenue and East 105th to pick up the latest pulps.

We both loved adventure, detective, and, most of all, science fiction magazines.

Other kids collected baseball cards, Jerry collected pulps. And he had a huge collection.

Even though Jerry lived in a bigger house, we would go to my place.

We were both huge fans of Hugo Gernsback's 'Amazing Stories.'

Frank Paul, who did the beautiful cover illustrations, was one of my favorite artists at the time.

The pulps were inspiration for my own art. I would trace Frank Paul's work, and then start creating my own.

Did you draw this?

Yes.

It's amazing!

Jerry loved to retell the stories he read, and then be inspired to invent his own.

It's the end of the Civil War and this Confederate soldier, John Carter, goes to Arizona where he finds gold.

But he runs afoul with the Apaches. They are chasing him.

He's trying to hide in a cave, but it turns out that this is a kind of sacred cave and somehow he is mysteriously transported to Mars.

On Mars, because of the lesser gravity, he has now superhuman strength; he can jump easily thirty feet high in the air, he can...

Jerry was a great storyteller. And he always had ideas.

See this empty bottle? Bet I could make up a story about that.

No doubt you could.

Did you know that Mary Shelley started writing Frankenstein when she was eighteen and the novel was published when she was twenty?

So you have to start working on your masterpiece.

I will, my friend, I will.

ha-ha-ha!

32

Jerry loved to write, no matter what season.

He corresponded with science fiction fans all over the U.S.

Jerry was, as he liked to point out, already a published author.

Well, an author of published letters to the editor, but nevertheless.

You can't be serious!

Why?

One of my favorite magazines was 'Physical Fitness.'

"We need stronger, more capable men.

"If your efforts are to be crowned with the halo of success, they must be spurred on the pulsating, throbbing powers that accompany physical excellence. These truly extraordinary characteristics come without effort to but few of us, but they can be developed, attained and maintained."

Bernarr Macfadden was one of my idols. I was a small, skinny kid but that didn't stop me from trying to improve myself.

HE MAKES HERCULES LOOK LIKE A SISSY!

MIGHTY

Jerry was a weekly contributor to the Torch, the Glenville High School newspaper. His 'Goober the Mighty,' a Tarzan parody, soon became a favorite among readers.

Another all-time favorite original Jerry creation was 'Stiletto Vance,' a funny pulp detective series.

Has anything been moved from the room?

Nothing, detective.

Can you investigate the storage room?

On my way.

⇒Hic!∈ Oh, boy Detective, how did you know ⇒hic∈ that the old lady had such good stuff here?

Because she isn't dead. I found a bottle of this stuff lying under her bed. The old lady ain't murdered, she's just drunk. Case closed!

Jerry convinced me to join the Torch as an illustrator.

Before I started working for the Torch, they had two beautiful girls working there. Lois Donaldson was the editor-in-chief. And then there was Maxine Kent, oh, what a beauty!

Did you talk to them?

Of course... not.

Where are my pencils?

Under there.

Where?

Under there.

Under where?

Ha, ha, he said underwear!

Very mature, gentleman.

Jerry encouraged me to participate in the Torch's Cartoon Contest.

Fresh off the press, my friend, fresh off the press. Look here.

And the winner is Joe Shuster! Beautiful work, my friend.

It was the first contest I had ever won. I was so proud.

Speaking of beauties, have you seen Little Angel?

I wrote a poem for her.

You did what?

I wrote a poem. And I am going to publish it in the Torch.

Jerry...

Lois
I think her eyes are wonderful,
I think her lips divine,
She's delicate as the chlorophyll,
Within a clinging vine.
I think her nose exquisite,
I think her chin sublime,
To think that we have never met,
Oh, what horrible crime!
She scarcely ever looks at me,
I worship every glance,
If she would only talk to me
I'd do a jubilant dance.
Oh, Lois, with your thoughtful eyes,
Cute nose and glorious lips,
I wonder if you realize
That you are my dream ship.

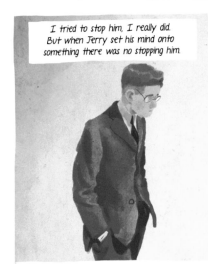

I tried to stop him, I really did. But when Jerry set his mind onto something there was no stopping him.

Needless to say, Lois Amster did not pay attention to him nor to the poem. But others did.

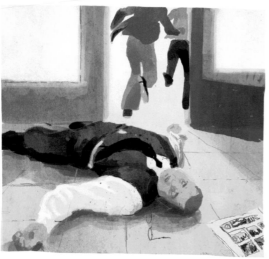

That summer, Jerry's father died.

39

Jerry did not want to talk about his father's death.

My mom felt very sorry for Jerry. We all did, but especially my mom.

My stories are as good as what's in these.

Why don't you submit some?

I am. Believe me, I am.

Jerry submitted his ideas to magazines, but the few answers he received were rejection letters.

Since no one wanted to publish Jerry's stories he decided to publish them himself using a mimeograph machine at school.

So we created our own magazine. It was called 'Science Fiction: The Advance Guard of Future Civilization.'

I drew the illustrations and most of the stories were written by Jerry using different pseudonyms.

The magazine was not bad, not bad at all.

Why are you wasting your talent with this?

At least we thought so.

My art teacher, Miss Bernstein, encouraged me to participate in the Cleveland Plain Dealer's annual Charity Football Poster Contest.

Every Thanksgiving weekend, the most important football game of the high school season was held at the Cleveland Municipal Stadium. The game was a fundraiser towards food baskets for the poor to be given out during Christmas.

And every year for the game the Plain Dealer ran an annual poster contest.

'Joseph Shuster, 18, of 10905 Amor Avenue NE yesterday was declared winner in the poster contest...'

"My parents were very proud.

'The judges worked for over three hours yesterday going over the entries. The first prize winner, they said, had produced a poster of excellent quality with attention, value and complete legibility.'

There was no money involved but 5,000 copies of my poster were printed and distributed all over Cuyahoga County.

Glenville
Charity Footba[l]

Did you see the poster?

I don't care about football.

I'm sorry. I didn't mean to-- I just had a bad day. Rejection letters, you know. But I'm happy for you, Joe, really.

I won two box seats to the game and took my brother with me.

Jerry had a new story idea for 'Science Fiction.'

There is a breadline. A row of disillusioned men. They are starving. Vagrants without hope.

Along comes a mad professor. He watches the men. The professor comes from a wealthy family. He never had to worry about anything.

The professor is watching the men. He reaches out to one of them, but then in the last moment hesitates. Then he does approach the raggedly-dressed man.

How would you like to have a real meal and a new suit?

What do you want me to do for you? Nothing crooked, I hope?

I assure you, my intentions are purely humanitarian.

The professor had previously secured a fragment of a meteor and during chemical analysis found... he suspects... a new element.

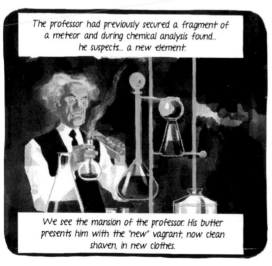

We see the mansion of the professor. His butler presents him with the 'new' vagrant, now clean shaven, in new clothes.

Look at you! What a transformation! It seems impossible that you are the same man!

Yes, it is possible for me to look respectable. Somehow it's hard for me to believe that you're doing this just out of the kindness of your heart.

This tastes so good. I haven't eaten for several days.

The professor has placed his chemical preparation into the coffee. The great experiment can begin.

I feel dizzy. I must have eaten too much.

Why don't you retire and we can talk tomorrow.

But the vagrant realizes what the professor has done and escapes.

But not only that. He has super-hearing and his vision... He can not only look up in the sky and see scenes on Mars as if they were just around the corner from him, no, he can also peek into the future and see how the stock market develops or know which horse will win the next race.

Time is simply duration, and duration is an illusion of the mind.

Nothing can stand in my way toward universal domination!

Intoxicated by his power, the vagrant uses his abilities for evil, seeks to rule the world. He returns to the professor and kills him so that no one else can gain these superpowers.

Just before he was murdered, the professor sent a letter to the editor of the city's main newspaper informing him about the experiment.

The editor sends his best man to investigate the story. He confronts the superman and is captured.

But then the powers wear off. The former vagrant realizes that now the professor is dead and no one can recreate the secret formula.

I see now how wrong I was. If I had worked for the good of humanity, my name would have gone down in history with a blessing instead of a curse.

He frees the reporter and has to return to the breadline. Once again he is the forgotten man he was at the beginning.

That's good, really good.

The story was called 'The Reign of the Super-Man' and was published in the third issue of 'Science Fiction'.

Little did we know that this was the beginning of creating a character that would become world-famous.

Science Fiction' discontinued soon after.

Jerry had big plans, big ideas, he made big announcements...

...but unfortunately, we had no big success... yet.

Jerry's next project idea.

Pulps in the form of comics!

That's where the money is. Writers of syndicated comics can make $1,000 per week, some headliners get even 50% of gross income. All we need is a unique idea!

This time I was not only illustrating stories written by Jerry. No, this time it was a real collaboration. We were literally sitting for hours in the same room, discussing ideas and creating this new magazine together. We called it 'Popular Comics.'

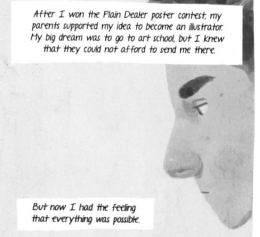

After I won the Plain Dealer poster contest, my parents supported my idea to become an illustrator. My big dream was to go to art school, but I knew that they could not afford to send me there.

But now I had the feeling that everything was possible.

Working on Popular Comics was a lot of fun.

BEEEP POW

SOME PAL HE IS! ALWAYS SMACKIN ME OVER TH HEAD AN TELLIN ME IT'S FOR MY OWN GOOD!

One of my favorite strips was 'Snoopy and Smiley,' who were a little bit like Laurel and Hardy.

At that time we were working for The Cleveland Shopping News, a popular coupon book.

Lemme do the talkin'.

Popular Comics is a good investment, you see. People love reading comics in the newspapers. Don't you love to read them yourself?

I do, yes. But how would this work?

See, these aren't reprints but totally new characters. And they come in the form of a magazine. Like the pulps, but with comics. It's a comic tabloid!

But who would pay for this?

It pays for itself. You see, it'll work like your coupon books. The kids will pick it up for the comics. At home, the parents will read them the stories - and also see the advertisements in the publication as well.

We couldn't believe it. The owner, Mr. Strong, said yes.

A contract! Signed! Fame, success, and big money just around the corner!

I can't believe he said yes.

SEE WHAT FAITH AND STICK-TO-IT-IVENESS CAN DO! JUST KEEP TRYING AND NEVER GIVE UP!

But our hopes died quickly. Mr. Strong changed his mind.

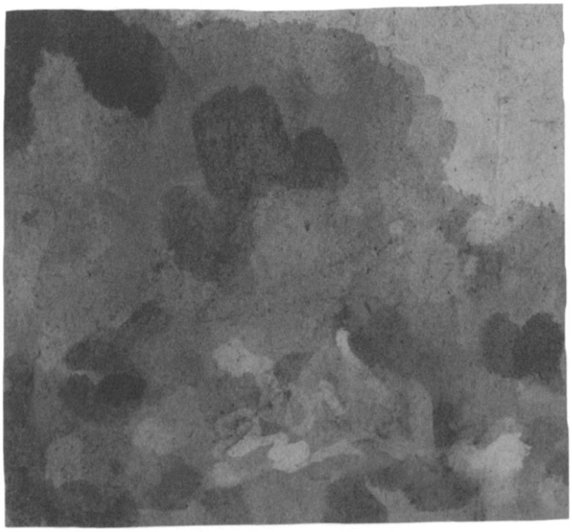
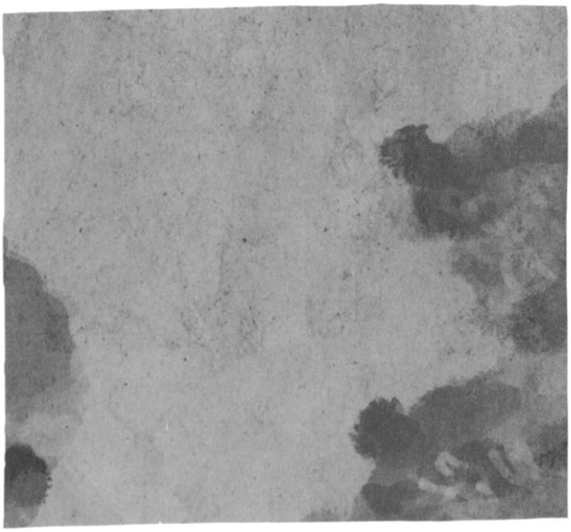
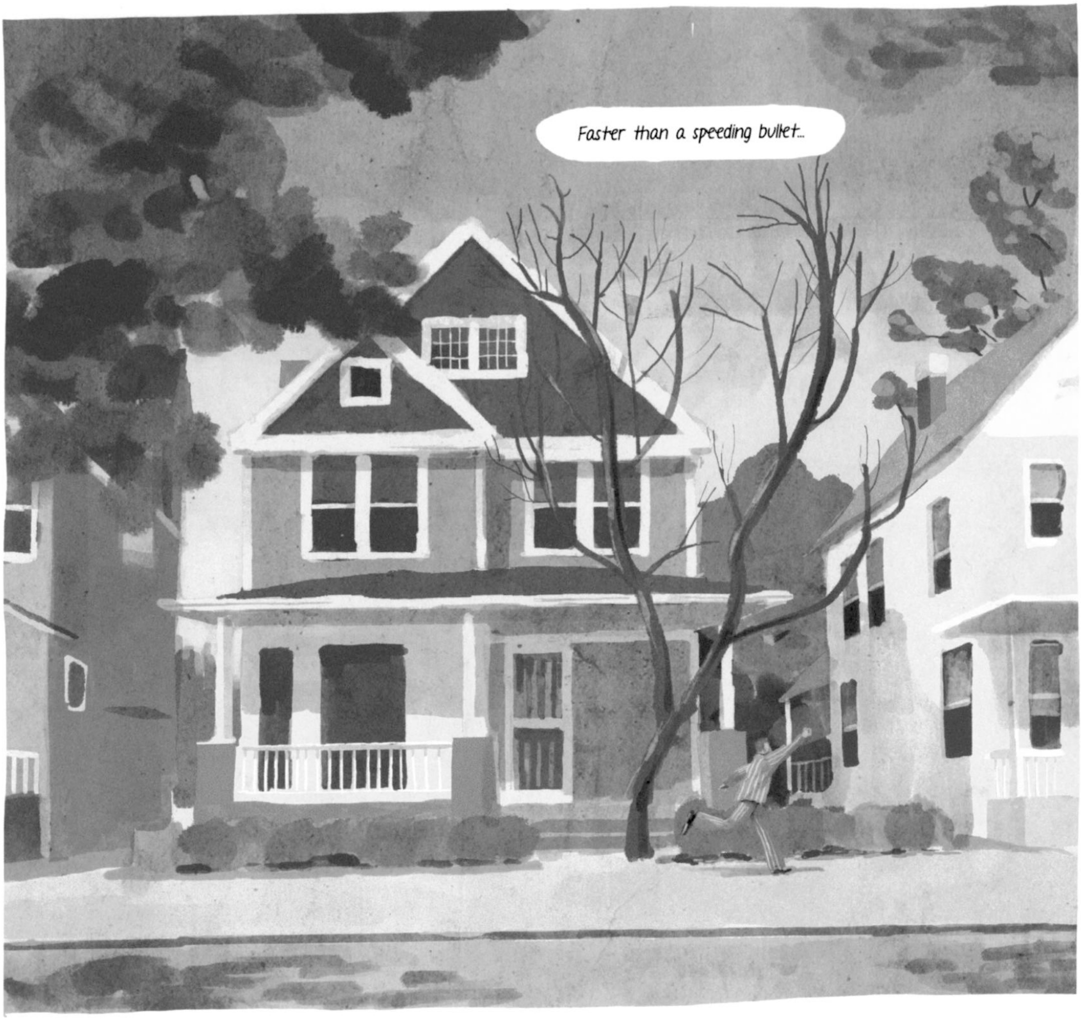
Faster than a speeding bullet...

Good morning, Mrs. Shuster. My apologies for being so early.

Did you have breakfast? Sit down, Jerry.

Good morning. What are you doing up so early?

Joe, we gotta talk. I got an idea.

You remember when I said that we need a unique idea? Something totally new? Something nobody has done yet?

Maybe.

I had this idea last night. It's something new. Something that doesn't exist yet. The Superman.

The story we did in Science Fiction?

Yes and no. He is now more like Flash Gordon or Buck Rogers, a real action hero. As a comic.

OK.

So he has all these powers, but he's now a crime-fighter.

Slow down and start at the beginning.

51

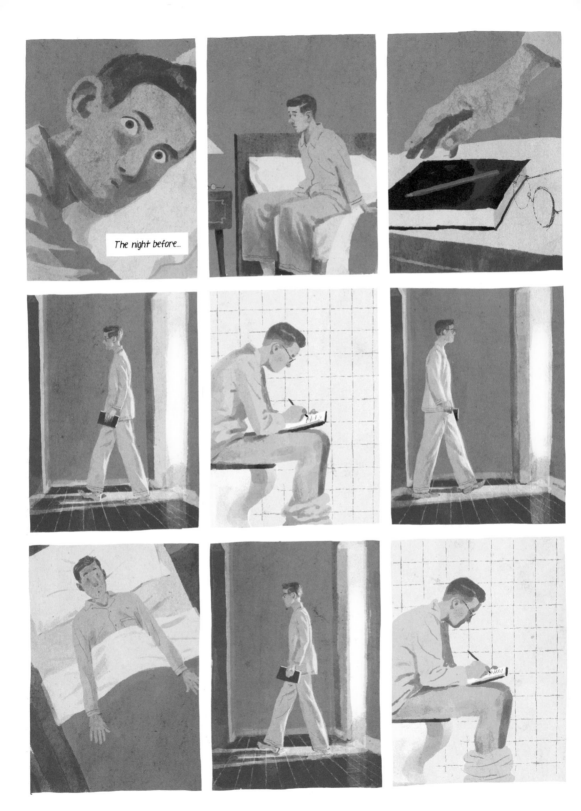

The night before...

So I hop right out of bed and write this down, and then I go back and think some more for about two hours and get up again and write that down.

This goes on all night, at two hour intervals, until in the morning I have a complete script.

We are in a distant future. Earth is doomed. So this scientist puts his infant son into a small time machine. In the moment Earth explodes, the vessel sparks back to the year... 1935.

So a man from the future travels back to our present.

Well, a baby from the future. But yes, correct. Someone finds the baby and places him in an orphanage. But because mankind advanced, the baby has superpowers.

Like what?

He can bend the bars of his crib, for example. There are lots of possibilities for humor.

I like that.

Unlike his predecessor in 'Science Fiction,' this Superman was using his powers to fight crime. It was science fiction, but the action was not happening in a distant future but in the here and now. Like Zorro, he had a secret identity, but he didn't wear a mask, only glasses that made him look like Harold Lloyd.

It was fun, it was adventure, it was new.

53

I got straight to work, using Jerry's notes to prepare some strips.

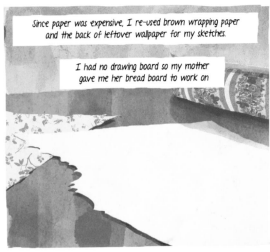

Since paper was expensive, I re-used brown wrapping paper and the back of leftover wallpaper for my sketches.

I had no drawing board so my mother gave me her bread board to work on

The board was made of wood with little side rails, and I would prop it up on the dining room table and draw.

Only on Friday my mother would take the board from me so that she could bake challah for Shabbat.

Look at this.

A STORY IN CARTOONS
DETECTIVE DAN
10¢

It's not Dick Tracy, but it's not bad. It's pretty good actually.

Geez-Louise, that's not the point.

So what is the point?

The point is that this is exactly what I had in mind. The point is that we can do this. You and me!

Do what?

Our own comic book. My ideas and your drawings. We can do this.

54

Jerry thought that the publisher would be interested in our strips. So we worked on a proposal for Humor Publication, the Chicago-based publisher of Detective Dan.

Look, it's you!

Let's call it 'a science fiction story in cartoons'— and in a box 'the most astounding fiction character of all time.'

A few months later we heard back from Humor Publication...

I got a letter.

And...?

I didn't open it. We'll open it together.

OK., so open it.

We have delayed in replying... until we could give... The Superman deliberate consideration... should we desire to put out another issue of Detective Dan... we then will be glad to take the matter up with you.

They were interested! They were really interested.

But there was never a second issue of Detective Dan.

Maybe it's time to move on.

Oh, boy, not again.

No, seriously, maybe it's just not meant to be.

I can do it with or without you!

A few weeks later.

Hey, Jerry!

Oh, hi!
How are you guys?

Haven't seen you in a while. Is everything O.K.?

Yeah, been busy.

What you got there?

Stuff.

What stuff?

Nothing important.

Why so mysterious? Show me!

I felt betrayed.

I gotta go. See you around.

Yeah, see you.

Superman was our project. We did it together. But apparently he decided to work with other artists. I wasn't good enough for him.

We graduated from Glenville High in June 1934.

Over the summer we hardly saw each other.

Then one day...

I brought you something.

What is it?

Look at it.

It was the same idea as Popular Comics, exactly what we had in mind, though Popular Comics was way better than this.

Oh, boy, don't you see?

Rats. Someone else did it.

See what?

Whereas I saw defeat, Jerry saw opportunity.

We can do this! You and me!

As a team!

And so we were back together... working on a proposal for the Major.

Malcolm Wheeler-Nicholson was called the Major because... well, because he was a major. He had served in the US Cavalry, was a decorated war hero.

The Major was a pulp writer with a life story of a pulp character.

He was said to have hunted down Pancho Villa, traveled to places as distant as Japan, and survived several assassination attempts – maybe not all his stories were true, but he was a good storyteller with a passion for writing.

In 1934, he founded 'National Allied Publications' and the following year 'New Fun' #1 was published. Now, the Major was looking for new work, and that's what we had to offer.

We sent him two proposals.

Henri Duval was a bit like the Three Musketeers: horses, cavaliers, pretty ladies. These kinds of stories were very popular at the time.

Doctor Occult was a detective with supernatural powers who was battling vampires, werewolves, and the like.

Maybe now was the time to revisit Superman.

Over the summer, Jerry had re-worked the script. Superman was no longer a time traveler, but journeyed from a different planet, giving a scientific explanation of his superpowers.

But something's still missing. I can feel it.

And then it dawned on us.

A girl!

Tarzan has Jane, and Superman has — Lois.

Really?

What?

Do you still have a crush on her? She never even talked to you.

What are you talking about?

Jerry, it's me you are talking to. Your best friend.

I just like the name. Lois, sounds like love...

O.K., guilty as charged.

60

What are you guys up to?

We're working.

Yes, I can see that.

O.K., so Tarzan has Jane, and Superman has Lois. But how would this work?

Well, as I mentioned, he is hiding his identity and works as a newspaper reporter, wears glasses...

You mean, he looks like you and me.

Exactly. So, maybe they work together. Hmm... Yes, Superman works for a newspaper and there is his female co-worker who hardly acknowledges him...

I wonder where you got this idea from...

But here comes the twist. She is in love with Superman, but she doesn't know that he is the same person.

Lois and...?

...Clark.

What?

Y'know, like the explorers. Lewis and Clark.

Lois and Clark. That's it. I like the sound of it.

So we had the idea. We had the name. Now we needed the sketches.

Jerry posed as Clark Kent.

For Superman, I used photos from my fitness magazines and posed in the mirror."

But I wasn't sure what to do about Lois. Jerry suggested to ask my sister, but I felt weird about it.

Then I saw an ad in the paper. A model looking for work.

Joe, you should write to her. You're an award-winning artist looking for a model for his upcoming cartoon strip.

I don't think she wants a cartoon artist to draw her.

I think she doesn't care as long as we pay.

But we don't have money for that.

You have to spend money to make money.

Why not? A model! A real model!

I don't know.

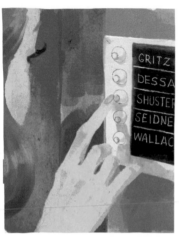

I'm the model that Mr. Shuster is expecting.

Come on in. Can I get you something? Water? Tea?

No, thank you. I'm fine. Can I leave my coat on? It's so cold today.

Absolutely. Once the session starts, you will take it off, right?

Of course. Just for now.

Yes, absolutely fine. Are you sure I can't get you anything?

Yeah, don't worry about it. I'm fine.

Sorry, what was your name again?

Oh, I'm sorry... Jolan.

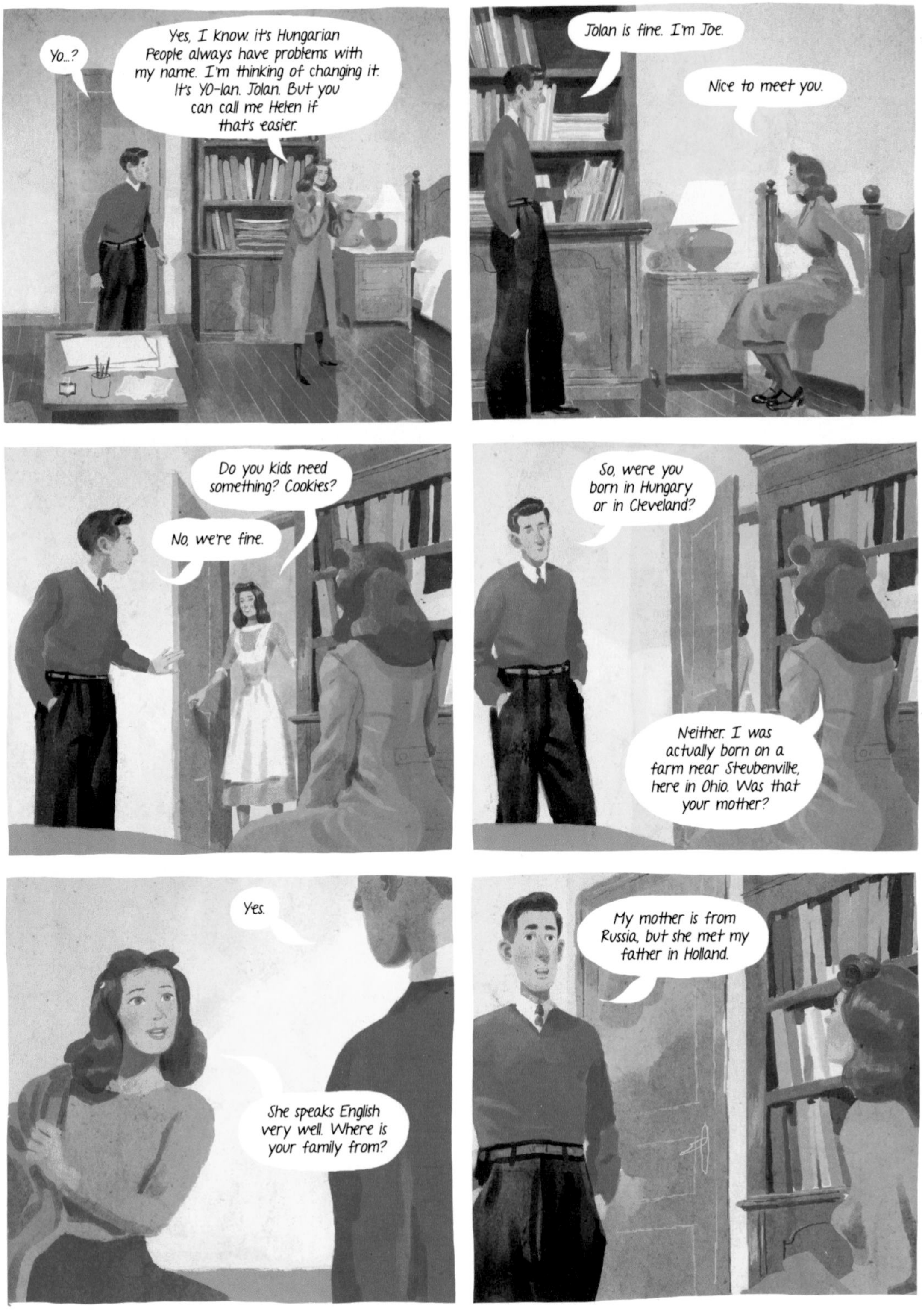
Yo...?
Yes, I know. it's Hungarian People always have problems with my name. I'm thinking of changing it. It's YO-lan. Jolan. But you can call me Helen if that's easier.
Jolan is fine. I'm Joe.
Nice to meet you.
Do you kids need something? Cookies?
No, we're fine.
So, were you born in Hungary or in Cleveland?
Neither. I was actually born on a farm near Steubenville, here in Ohio. Was that your mother?
Yes.
She speaks English very well. Where is your family from?
My mother is from Russia, but she met my father in Holland.

And you were born here?

No, in Toronto. We lived there until I was nine.

I've never been there but I heard that it's a great city.

I guess so. I go back there every summer and stay with my aunt and uncle.

You have siblings?

Yes, a younger brother and a younger sister.

We're six, all girls.

So how did you come to Cleveland?

Well, my parents hardly speak any English. And my father lost his farm because of some misunderstandings. Long story. So he moved the family to Cleveland to work in a steel mill.

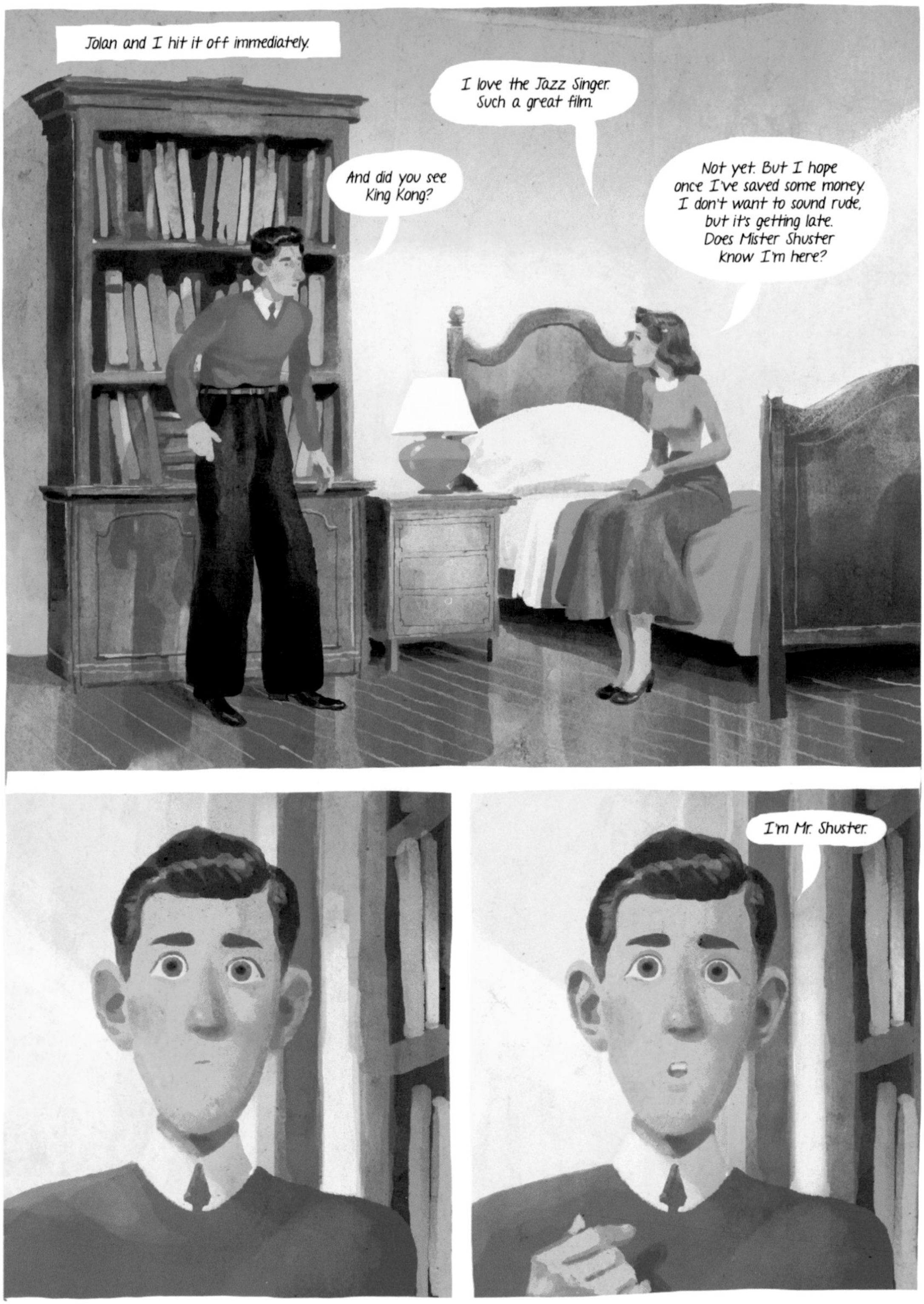
Jolan and I hit it off immediately.
And did you see King Kong?
I love the Jazz Singer. Such a great film.
Not yet. But I hope once I've saved some money. I don't want to sound rude, but it's getting late. Does Mister Shuster know I'm here?
I'm Mr. Shuster.

Where is she?

In the bathroom. She's changing into her bathing suit.

How does she look?

Good.

Good?

She's cute. Beautiful. A real beauty.

Don't say this before you have seen her in her bathing suit.

Jerry! She can probably hear you.

I can't believe you actually did this.

But you told me we should?

Yes, but I didn't believe you'd do it.

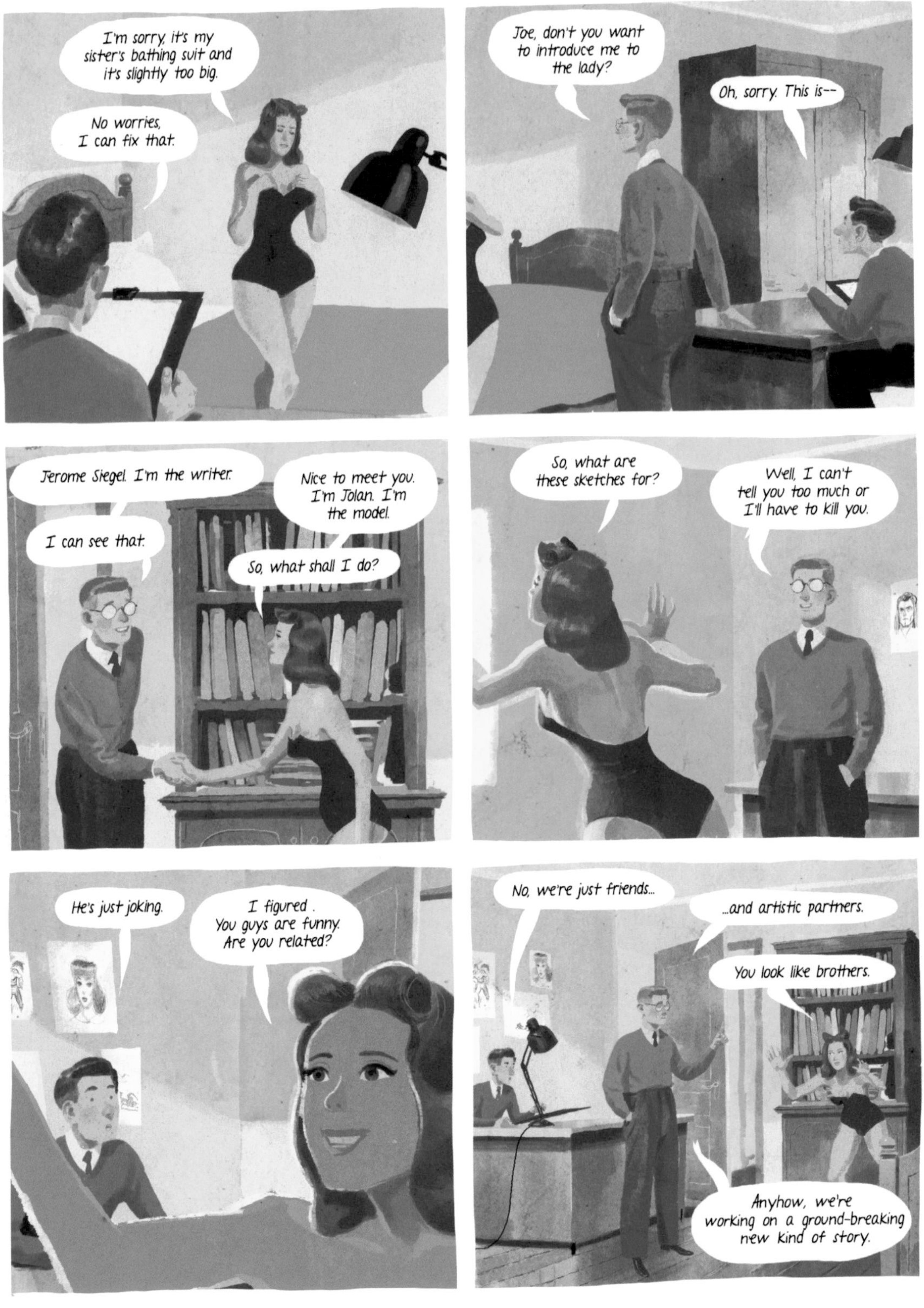
I'm sorry, it's my sister's bathing suit and it's slightly too big.
No worries, I can fix that.
Joe, don't you want to introduce me to the lady?
Oh, sorry. This is--
Jerome Siegel. I'm the writer.
I can see that.
Nice to meet you. I'm Jolan. I'm the model.
So, what shall I do?
So, what are these sketches for?
Well, I can't tell you too much or I'll have to kill you.
He's just joking.
I figured . You guys are funny. Are you related?
No, we're just friends...
...and artistic partners.
You look like brothers.
Anyhow, we're working on a ground-breaking new kind of story.

Jerry went on and on about Superman.

You're going to be famous, I can feel it.

So next week, same time same place?

Yes, I think we have do so some more sketches and try some more poses.

Oh...

Sure, yes, I'm available.

Jolan came for a few more sessions to my home. Sometimes Jerry joined us, sometimes he didn't.

We even went out a few times.
I guess we kind of dated.

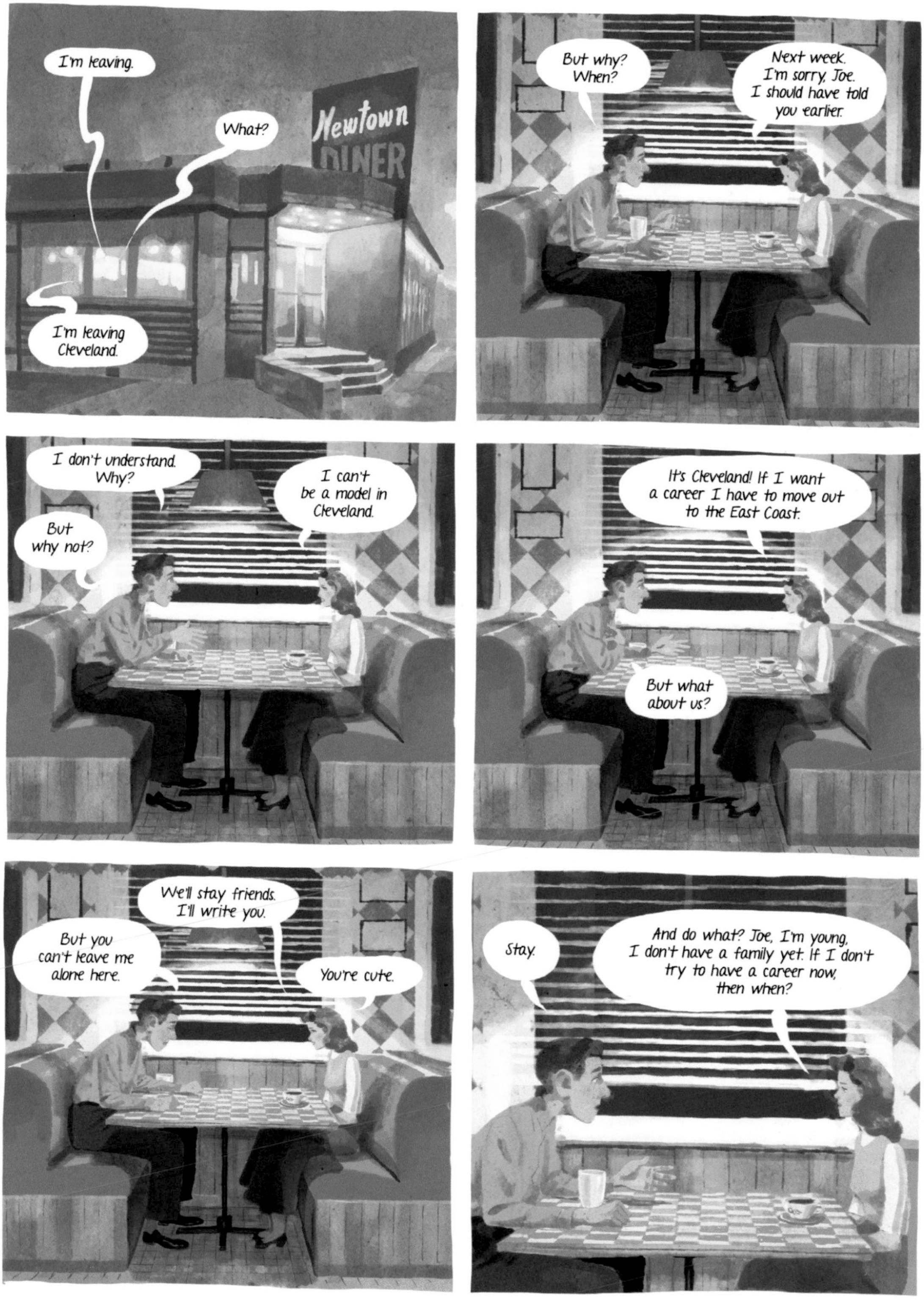
I'm leaving.
What?
I'm leaving Cleveland.
Newtown DINER
But why? When?
Next week. I'm sorry, Joe. I should have told you earlier.
I don't understand. Why?
I can't be a model in Cleveland.
But why not?
It's Cleveland! If I want a career I have to move out to the East Coast.
But what about us?
We'll stay friends. I'll write you.
But you can't leave me alone here.
You're cute.
Stay.
And do what? Joe, I'm young, I don't have a family yet. If I don't try to have a career now, then when?

And she kept her promise. She kept in touch. She wrote, in the beginning nearly every week, then every few months.

Another crime-stopping series was 'Radio Squad,' a feature about a policeman, Sandy Kean, who drove a patrol car with a police radio. Back then, this was an innovation.

'Federal Men' was inspired by James Cagney movies and had its debut in New Comics #2, a second magazine published by the Major. The hero was FBI agent Steve Carson, and Jerry based the first episode, 'The Manning Baby Kidnapping,' on the infamous kidnapping of Lindbergh's son.

And then there was 'Spy,' a feature about the secret agent Bart Regan and his fiancée Sally Norris, two counter-espionage agents for the U.S. government, and their globetrotting adventures.

The stories were usually two pages, the typical length of a series in 'More Fun Comics,' and also the typical length of a Sunday comic strip page.

73

Slam was the Major's idea, but it would become our creation.

SLAM BRADLEY

by JEROME SIEGEL Y JOE SHUSTER

"THERE WERE NO RESTRICTIONS. WE HAD THE COMPLETE FREEDOM TO DO WHAT WE WANTED THE ONLY PROBLEM WAS WE HAD A DEADLINE.

"WE HAD TO WORK VERY FAST, SO JERRY SUGGESTED WE SAVE TIME BY PUTTING LESS THAN SIX PANELS ON A PAGE.

CRUNCH

THE KIDS LOVED IT BECAUSE IT WAS SPECTACULAR. I COULD DO SO MUCH MORE.

"LATER ON THE EDITORS STOPPED US FROM DOING THAT.

"THEY SAID THE KIDS WERE..

NOT GETTING THEIR MONEY'S WORTH.

74

I brought you some cookies and cocoa.

Thank you, Mrs. Shuster.

You boys work too hard.

Well, we have lots to do.

I'm happy to see you and Joe succeeding.

But...?

But where's the money?

The Major was often late with the payments.

We were tremendously proud to see our work in print month after month after month, but we hardly made a living.

During the day, I worked delivery jobs. then came home, ate dinner and, at night, I read Jerry's scripts and worked on my drawings.

I left the business side to Jerry. He was the one communicating with the Major in New York, he was the one creating the scripts for the stories, and he was also the one looking for other job opportunities.

We sold two cartoons to the Cleveland District Golfer for $7.50, the advertising company will pay us $10 for the layouts, and there is an offer to create Valentine's Cards for $15.

That summer, Berlin was hosting the Olympic Games. There had been some debate here whether the United States should boycott the games or not. Germany had been selected as host country before Adolf Hitler and the Nazi Party rose to power.

In the end, we didn't boycott the games because of Avery Brundage, the leader of U.S. Olympic Committee.

Brundage believed that a 'Jewish-Communist conspiracy' was behind the call for a boycott.

THE VERY FOUNDATION OF THE MODERN OLYMPIC REVIVAL WILL BE UNDERMINED IF INDIVIDUAL COUNTRIES ARE ALLOWED TO RESTRICT PARTICIPATION BY REASON OF CLASS, CREED, OR. ...

RACE

In 1934, Brundage went on a facts-finding mission to Germany and ascertained that German Jews were being treated fairly. After all, he belonged to a sports club in Chicago that did not allow Jews entry, either.

The Nazis wanted to use the Olympic Games to promote their ideas of Aryan Superiority. You cannot imagine how proud we were when a local boy, Jesse Owens, won four gold medals.

Owens was originally from Alabama, but his family moved to Cleveland around the same time as we did. He attended Ohio State and after he won a record eight individual college championships, they called him 'Buckeye Bullet.'

We did not forget about Superman. Even with all the other work we were doing, we still hoped that one day our idea would be syndicated as a newspaper strip.

It is my idea, based on my experience in selling the syndicate game, that you would be much better off doing Superman in full page in four colors for one of our publications.

MAJOR MALCOLM WHEELER NICHOLSON

The potential of the character, Superman, has barely been scratched... He's different and sure to become the idol of young and old.

Unlike most adventure strips, the scene of the story will not be laid in some fantastic, unknown jungle or planet or country, but will be all the more astounding for having a locale on familiar streets.

Superman will operate against the backdrop of America's well-known cities, buildings, and pleasure spots.'

No one was interested.

We were ready to give up, but then everything changed.

"The trouble with Superman is that it is still a rather immature piece of work. It is attractive because of its freshness and naivete, but this is likely to wear off after the feature runs for a whi

New York, 1937.

I love it!

Really?

That is Sheldon Mayer, who worked with the Major at National Allied Publications since its inception, and also joined McClure Syndicate, where he worked for Maxwell Charles Gaines. In 1933, Gaines had devised the four-color, saddle-stitched newsprint pamphlet, a precursor for the color comics format that would later become the standard for the comic book industry.

What do you think, Max?

It's different, Shelly.

I'm crazy about Superman for the same reason I liked "The Scarlet Pimpernel," "Zorro," and "The Desert Song." The mystery man and his alter ego are two distinct characters to be played off against each other.

The Scarlet Pimpernel's alter ego was scared of the sight of blood, a hopeless dandy: no one would have suspected he was a hero. The same goes for Superman.

That night, Sheldon invited us for dinner. He was the first person who believed in Superman. He gave us hope.

McClure Syndicate, M.C. Gaines speaking.

Sheldon Mayer here. How are you, Ginsberg?

Shelly! Long time no see. How can I help you?

Well, I got big news.

You went on a date?

Haha! Even bigger. Donenfeld and Sampliner have taken over.

Get outta here! What about The Major?

He's out.

That is big news!

Told ya!

So how can I help you?

Well, they are looking for unpublished strips for a new comic book.

We got plenty of these. I will have a messenger bring over a whole bunch of unused strips.

Do you remember the one from these two guys from Cleveland?

Sure do.

Make sure it's among them.

We should publish this one.

Whatever you think, Shelly. Just show it to Jack, will ya?

I have some strips for the new comic book.

And?

Harry said you should take a look at it.

Just show them to Vin.

VINCENT SULLIVAN

Cleveland, January, 1938.

Are these the new scripts?

Yes, and I got mail from Sullivan.

Vin Sullivan was our editor at Nicholson Publications. In January, 1938, he informed us that someone had taken over the company and that the Major was out.

'The one feature I like best, and the one that seems to fit into the proposed schedule is that Superman.'

They were interested in publishing Superman and wanted 13 pages for their news publication 'Action Comics.'

I dunno.

I think we should give it a try. And syndication might follow.

You think so?

Trust me. I have a good feeling about it.

And so it happened. We had waited so long for this moment, and now, finally, Superman would be published.

Sullivan sent us back our Superman sample strips and we cut and pasted them into 13 comic book pages and mailed them back to New York.

I, the undersigned, am an artist or author and have performed work for strip entitled SUPERMAN. In consideration of $130.00 agreed to be paid me by you, I hereby sell and transfer such work and strip, all good will attached thereto and exclusive right to the use of the characters and story, continuity and title of strip contained therein, to you and your assigns to have and hold forever and to be your exclusive property and I agree not to employ said characters by their names contained therein or under any other names at any time hereafter to any other person firm or cooperation, or permit the use thereof by said other parties without obtaining your written consent thereof. The intent hereof is to give you exclusive right to use and acknowledge that you own said characters or story and the use thereof, exclusively. I have received the above sum of money.

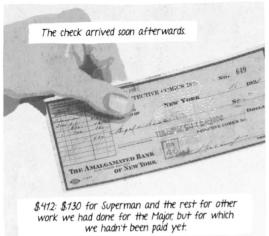

The check arrived soon afterwards.

$412: $130 for Superman and the rest for other work we had done for the Major, but for which we hadn't been paid yet.

We were positively surprised by the quick turn-around. Whoever took over from the Major, they made a positive first impression.

Wow, that was quick.

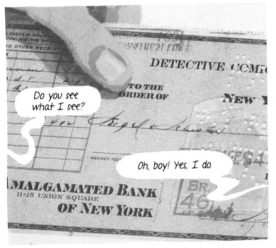

Do you see what I see?

Oh, boy! Yes, I do.

Yes, so, uhm, we are the recipients, but, uhm, both our names are spelled incorrectly.

Please wait here, I'll be back in a moment.

Can I see a form of identification?

So who is Mister Siegel? And who is Mister Shuster?

Well, there are not so many more options.

So the check is made out to Seigel - spelled S-E-I - and Schuster - spelled S-C-H. What we have to do is the following: You sign the check the way it is spelled on the check, and then, next to it, with your correctly spelled names.

Thank you.

April.

Oh, what's this?

Looks very interesting!

Yes, it does. This Samson lifting the car. I think I'm gonna buy this.

Yeah, me, too. Love the artwork.

Why does it say June on the cover if it's published in April?

Mrs. Shuster, this is modern marketing. If the publication does not sell out, it still looks fresh on the newsstand in a few weeks from now.

I see.

Well, I'm proud of you, boys.

Vendors have sold around 130,000 copies of Action Comics #1. The print-run was 202,000 copies, so 64% was sold.

That's good?

Anything over 50% is a success.

In New York, the publishers tried to figure out who was driving the sales. They had printed 20,000 promotional posters for newsstands, pharmacies, corner stores, groceries, bus stops and train stations. They had arranged for Action Comics #1 to stay on the shelves for six weeks, rather than the standard four.

Out of Action Comics's 64 pages, only 13 were Superman. But it was Superman the kids wanted, not Zatara Master Magician, Sticky-Mitt Stimson or any of the other eight features.

Do you have the magazine with the...

Superman. The one with Superman.

Oh, yes, Action Comics. Yes, it's this one over here.

Jerry and I would go to the newsstand and watch kids asking for Superman, Wednesday after Wednesday after Wednesday.

Superman was selling well, very well.

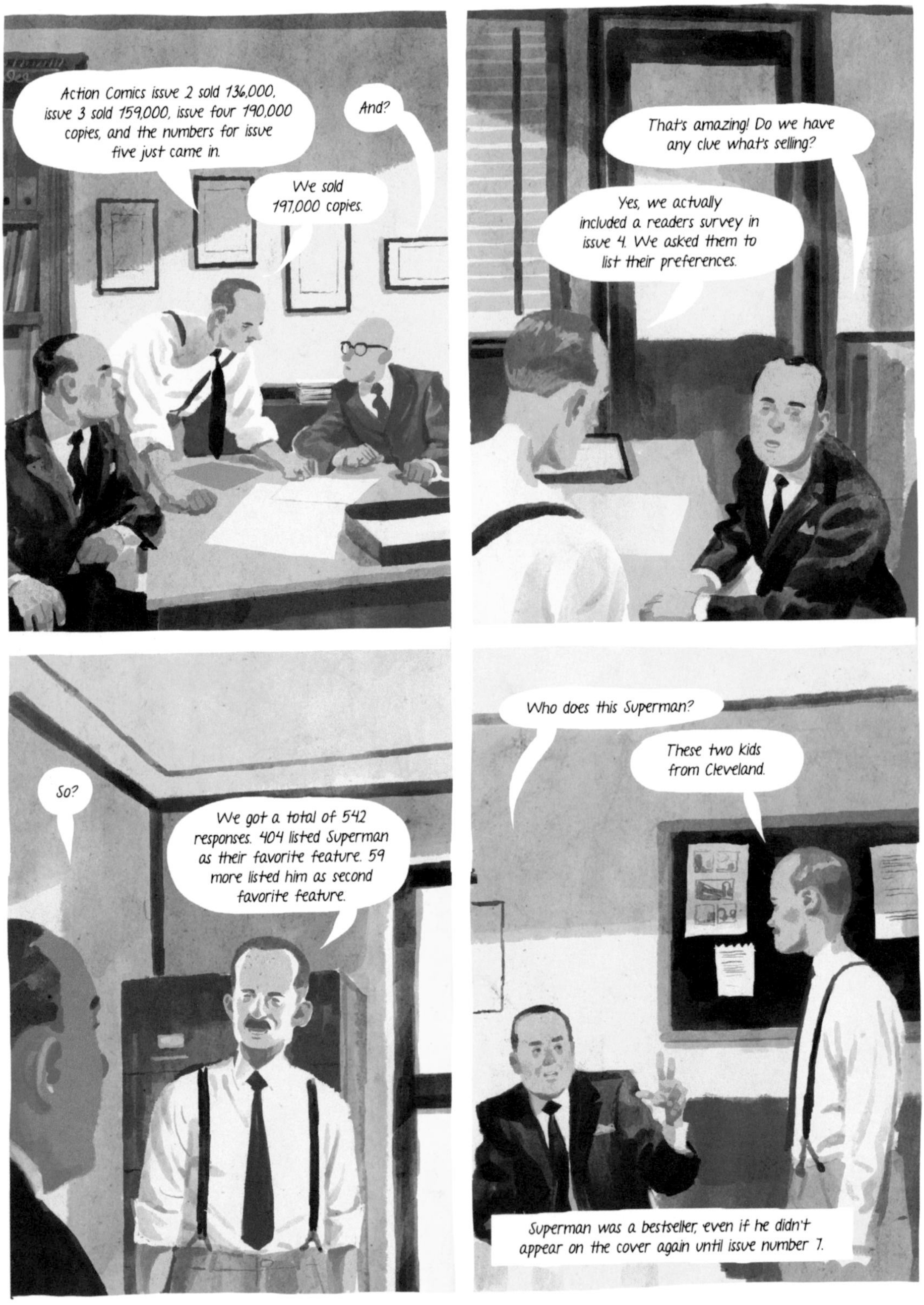
Action Comics issue 2 sold 136,000, issue 3 sold 159,000, issue four 190,000 copies, and the numbers for issue five just came in.
And?
We sold 197,000 copies.
That's amazing! Do we have any clue what's selling?
Yes, we actually included a readers survey in issue 4. We asked them to list their preferences.
So?
We got a total of 542 responses. 404 listed Superman as their favorite feature. 59 more listed him as second favorite feature.
Who does this Superman?
These two kids from Cleveland.
Superman was a bestseller, even if he didn't appear on the cover again until issue number 7.

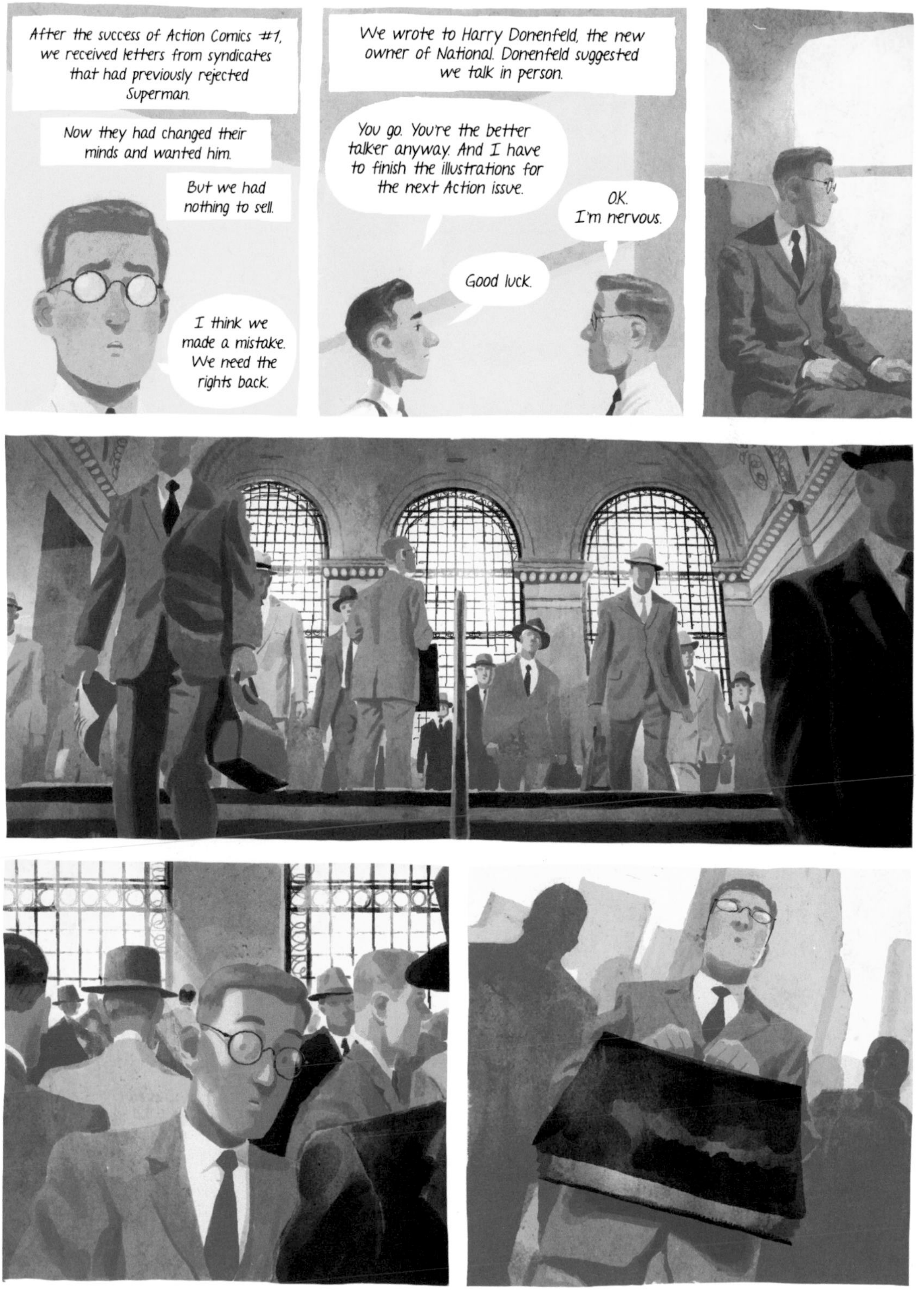
After the success of Action Comics #1, we received letters from syndicates that had previously rejected Superman.
Now they had changed their minds and wanted him.
But we had nothing to sell.
I think we made a mistake. We need the rights back.
We wrote to Harry Donenfeld, the new owner of National. Donenfeld suggested we talk in person.
You go. You're the better talker anyway. And I have to finish the illustrations for the next Action issue.
OK. I'm nervous.
Good luck.

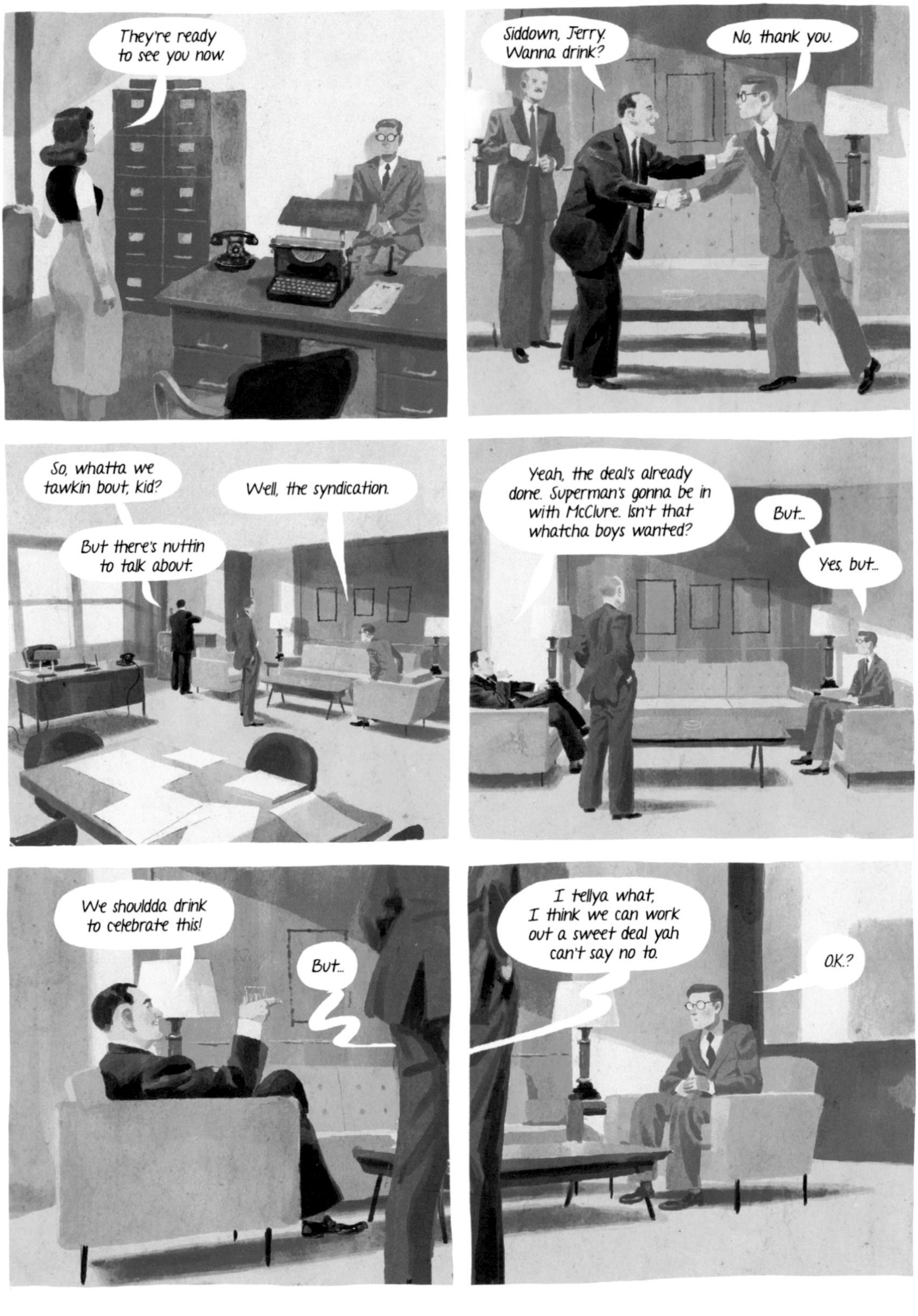
They're ready to see you now.
Siddown, Jerry. Wanna drink?
No, thank you.
So, whatta we tawkin bout, kid?
Well, the syndication.
But there's nuttin to talk about.
Yeah, the deal's already done. Superman's gonna be in with McClure. Isn't that whatcha boys wanted?
But...
Yes, but...
We shouldda drink to celebrate this!
But...
I tellya what, I think we can work out a sweet deal yah can't say no to.
O.K.?

So, here's what we do. If you and your friend sign a ten-year deal, you can do the newspaper strips and get some of the royalties.

I dunno.

Jack, what'dja think?

I think this sounds fair. Legally, I have to remind you, National owns all the rights to the Superman feature.

But it's ours.

Well, you created it. We own it. You kids sold it to us. A deal's a deal.

But...

It states here very clearly, signed by you and Shuster, dated March 1, 1938 and returned by mail on March 3, 1938 that you, and I quote, 'hereby sell and transfer such work and strip—

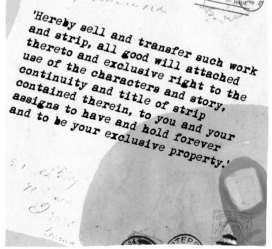

'Hereby sell and transfer such work and strip, all good will attached thereto and exclusive right to the use of the characters and story, continuity and title of strip contained therein, to you and your assigns to have and hold forever and to be your exclusive property.'

91

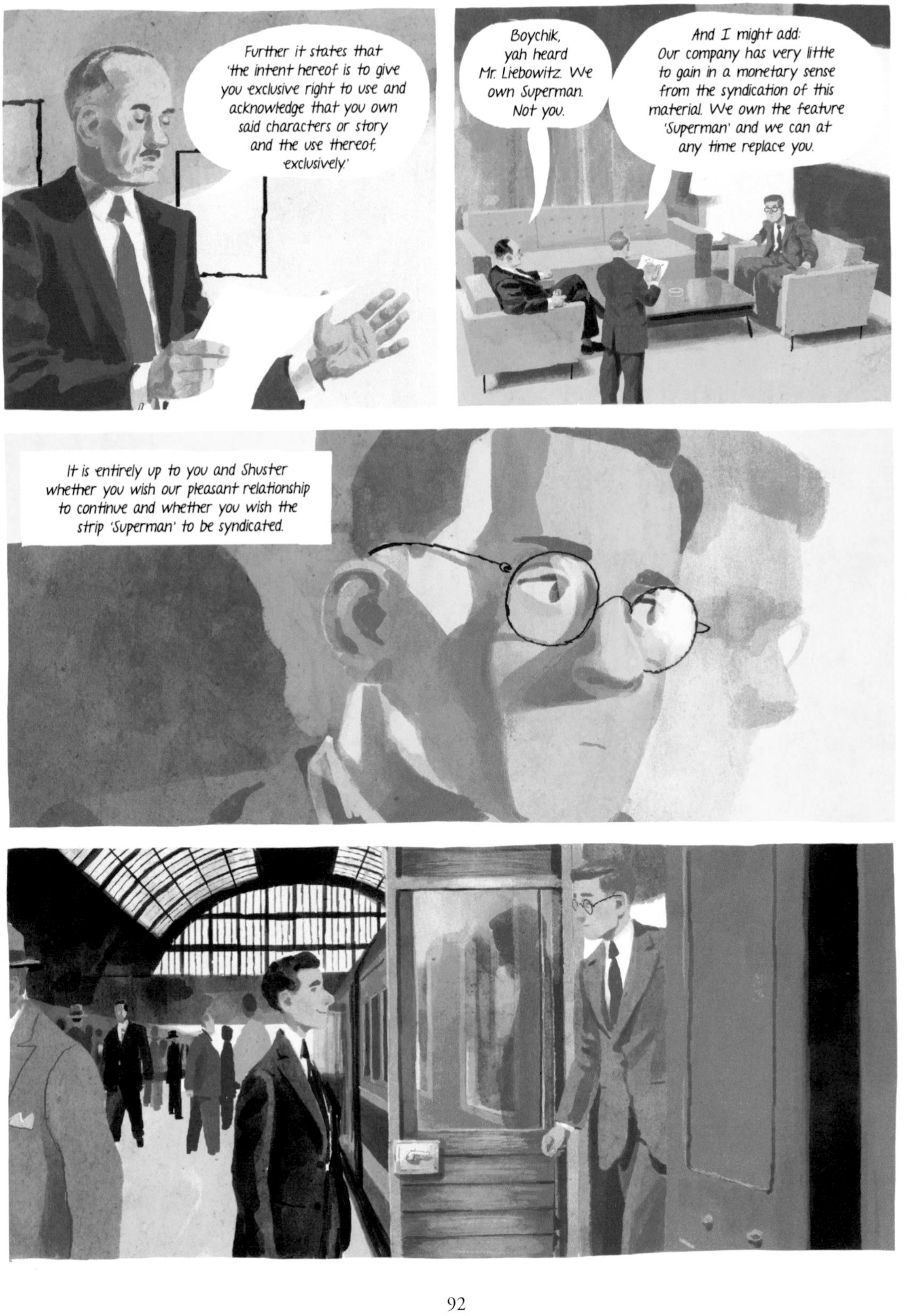
Further it states that 'the intent hereof is to give you exclusive right to use and acknowledge that you own said characters or story and the use thereof, exclusively.'
Boychik, yah heard Mr. Liebowitz. We own Superman. Not you.
And I might add: Our company has very little to gain in a monetary sense from the syndication of this material. We own the feature 'Superman' and we can at any time replace you.
It is entirely up to you and Shuster whether you wish our pleasant relationship to continue and whether you wish the strip 'Superman' to be syndicated.

Superman began syndication on January 16, 1939. The Houston Chronicle was the first paper to publish a daily Superman strip, followed by the Milwaukee Journal and the San Antonio Express. By the end of 1939, sixty papers were running a daily Superman feature and a Sunday strip.

Soon McClure Syndicate placed Superman in hundreds of daily papers and 90 Sunday papers - over 20 Million people were reading Superman.

We printed 725,000 copies of Action Comics, 16,625,000 were sold. That is a success rate of 86%.

To us! And these two boychicks from Cleveland!

In June, Superman became the first feature to have his own comic book named after him. Actually, it was meant to be only a one time issue with reprints and a behind the scenes portrait of us.

The first press run of Superman - half a million copies - sold out. Then a second printing of 250,000 additional copies sold out as well, and then nearly all of the 150,000 copies of the third printing.

NATIONAL COMICS 10¢

So National decided to make Superman a quarterly magazine.

It was insane. Everybody wanted Superman.

It didn't take long for copycats to create their knockoffs. Only a few months after Superman's debut, Victor Fox hired Will Eisner.

I want another Superman!

Eisner created Wonder Man in less than a week. His powers are almost exactly like Superman's.

The moment the issue saw print, National sued Fox for copyright infringement. Wonder Man only saw one issue.

I am the king of comics!

But this did not stop Fox, who had other artists create other knockoffs like the Flame, the Blue Beetle, or the Green Mask.

And he was not the only one who created their own Superman.

No doubt, we had created a blueprint for a new genre: The costume, especially the cape, the dual identity, the superpowers, even the fact that superheroes were living in big cities, this all came from Superman.

We caused a total superhero boom. And everybody wanted a piece of the cake. It was unavoidable.

So National and its spin off company All-American started introducing their own superhero features.

With every new superhero introduced, Jerry got more nervous.

Superman won't last forever, and then what?

I don't understand why they're introducing all these other features? They're taking away sales from Superman.

Well...

How many features do we need? There's only one Superman!

As much as Jerry didn't like other superheroes, there was one in particular he disliked:

I hate the Batman.

Get me a new Superman by Monday.

On a Friday afternoon in late '38, Vin Sullivan had asked contributors for ideas for a new costumed hero

So Bob Kane came up with Batman. Or, as we later found out, he and his friend Bill Finger did, even if he never got the credit he deserved.

Finger did most of the writing, Jerry Robinson did most of the drawing, but Bob got all the credit.

The strange thing was that Bob always denied that anyone but him did Batman, which was, of course, absurd. National was giving all of us more work than we could possibly handle.

We all needed help.

We rented an upstairs studio on Euclid Avenue, near East 105th Street, and hired a bunch of artists to help us with inking and lettering.

We called our studio 'The Shuster Shop'

Jerry refused to have help. He wanted to do it all by himself. Jerry wrote the scripts for the daily strips and the Sunday strips.

Monthly stories for Action Comics and the Superman magazine.

He also wrote the two-page Superman short stories.

The U.S. Postal Service had a rule that a magazine has to have at least two consecutive pages of text to be eligible for a cheaper mailing rate. So I wrote these little pulp stories about Superman that were included in the magazines.

Jerry was actually in good company. At Timely Comics, Stanley Lieber was writing these features.

Timely later changed its name to Marvel Comics, and Lieber changed his to Stan Lee.

I honestly don't think anyone was reading these stories.

In the beginning, we had a free hand to do whatever we wanted. But once it became clear that Superman was big business, New York had to approve all the plots. Less social crusading, less guns and knives, and most importantly, Superman was only allowed to use his superpowers in costume.

Jerry did not only write Superman. He was still doing Slam Bradley, Federal Men, Spy, Radio Squad, and he came up with a new feature: The Spectre.

The Spectre was a different kind of superhero. This green hooded fighter was a former detective, murdered and then brought back from the afterlife by a mysterious light that gave him powers to wreak vengeance.

In New York, Donenfeld and Liebowitz were not convinced about this new feature. They even came to Cleveland to talk him out of it.

All we want you to do is write Superman. Forget Slam Bradley and the other features, just focus on Superman.

Look, I'm gonna write it all! I can do it.

Lissen, boychik, we got something goin' here. It's working. I don't understand how or why, but it's working. Why change it? We're all getting paid.

If it's about the money, as Mister Donenfeld and I have discussed, we can pay you more money so that you can focus on the existing formula...

Yeah, kid. Why risk losing our readers?

No. I can do it. Trust me. I know what I'm doing.

School's over. She must be coming home.

Despite the success of Superman, we were still two boys from Glenville, living with our parents, but Superman gave us superpowers...

...or at least a self-esteem boost.

Jerry started dating Bella Lifshitz, a girl who lived across the street from him.

He was happy.

His mother was not.

Bella Lifshitz!? Of all people he has to go out with that girl.

Jerry's mom knew Bella's parents from shul.

Bella's father was a plumber.

He fixes toilets and unclogs sinks for a living!

And Bella's mother spoke little English.

She still lives in Yiddishland!

Maybe she was just afraid of being alone.
Jerry was the youngest, still living at home.

No, she's only going after your money!

That's absurd.

She's too young!

She's 18!

If you marry her I'll die!

They got married in June, a week after Bella graduated high school.

Jerry and Bella first lived on Cloverside Avenue, but Bella wanted a bigger house in a better area. So they looked at University Heights, which was becoming the new Jewish neighborhood.

Welcome to
University
Heights

I found a place on Tyndall. You should move there, too. Why are you staying in Glenville? You earn now enough money to move out.

It's called the American Dream!

I was actually considering finding a new house for my parents. Sometimes I think this is all a dream.

I purchased a house for my parents on Ivydale Road, ten minutes away from Jerry and Bella.. Only Jerry's mother stayed behind in Glenville, and she refused to set foot in... 'any house kept by that girl!'

Let me give you the grand tour, my friend!

IT MUST HAVE BEEN MOONGLOW, WAY UP IN THE BLUE
IT MUST HAVE BEEN MOONGLOW THAT LED ME STRAIGHT TO YOU

I STILL HEAR YOU SAYIN', 'SWEET CHILD, HOLD ME FAST'
AND I KEEP ON PRAYIN', 'OH, LORD, PLEASE LET THIS LAST'

Even if Jerry was now a married man, he was still the same kid I'd known in high school.

On February 12, 1940, Superman debuted on NYC's WOR 710 AM.

The radio show was 15 minutes long and ran several times a week.

It was the brainchild of Allen 'Duke' Ducovny, National's new publicist.

Even if Jerry wanted to do it, Robert Maxwell was the one writing the scripts for the radio show. Jerry was angry, but Donenfeld knew how to keep us happy. He was very good at that.

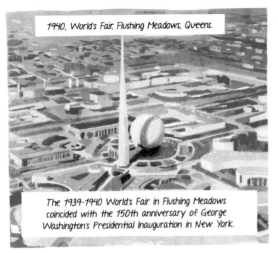

1940, World's Fair, Flushing Meadows, Queens.

The 1939-1940 World's Fair in Flushing Meadows coincided with the 150th anniversary of George Washington's Presidential Inauguration in New York.

Ladies and gentlemen, Solomon, the Human Torch. A true hell diver!

Over 45 million visitors were introduced to modern marvels such as color photography and air conditioning.

I gotta see Johnny Weissmuller! That's so exciting!

Donenfeld and Liebowitz, businessmen as they were, decided to cash in on the fair.

National printed a special 'World's Fair Comics,' which featured a Superman story set at the Fair, but also Slam Bradley and other characters. The issue sold out on opening day, April 30, 1939.

The following year, a new issue of 'World's Fair Comics' with new adventures was published, this time featuring also Batman.

I hate Batman!

But that wasn't all. July 3, 1940 was declared Superman Day at the World's Fair... another idea by National publicist Ducovny."

Wow! Charles Atlas will be at the award ceremony!

Who?

Charles Atlas from MacFadden's 'Physical Culture' magazine!

Kids were encouraged to dress as Superman and participate in a bunch of activities promoting physical fitness.

It was strange.

But it became even stranger when the parade started.

First, there was Harry Donenfeld on an elephant...

Look at this clown!

...and then...

...well, then there was Superman.

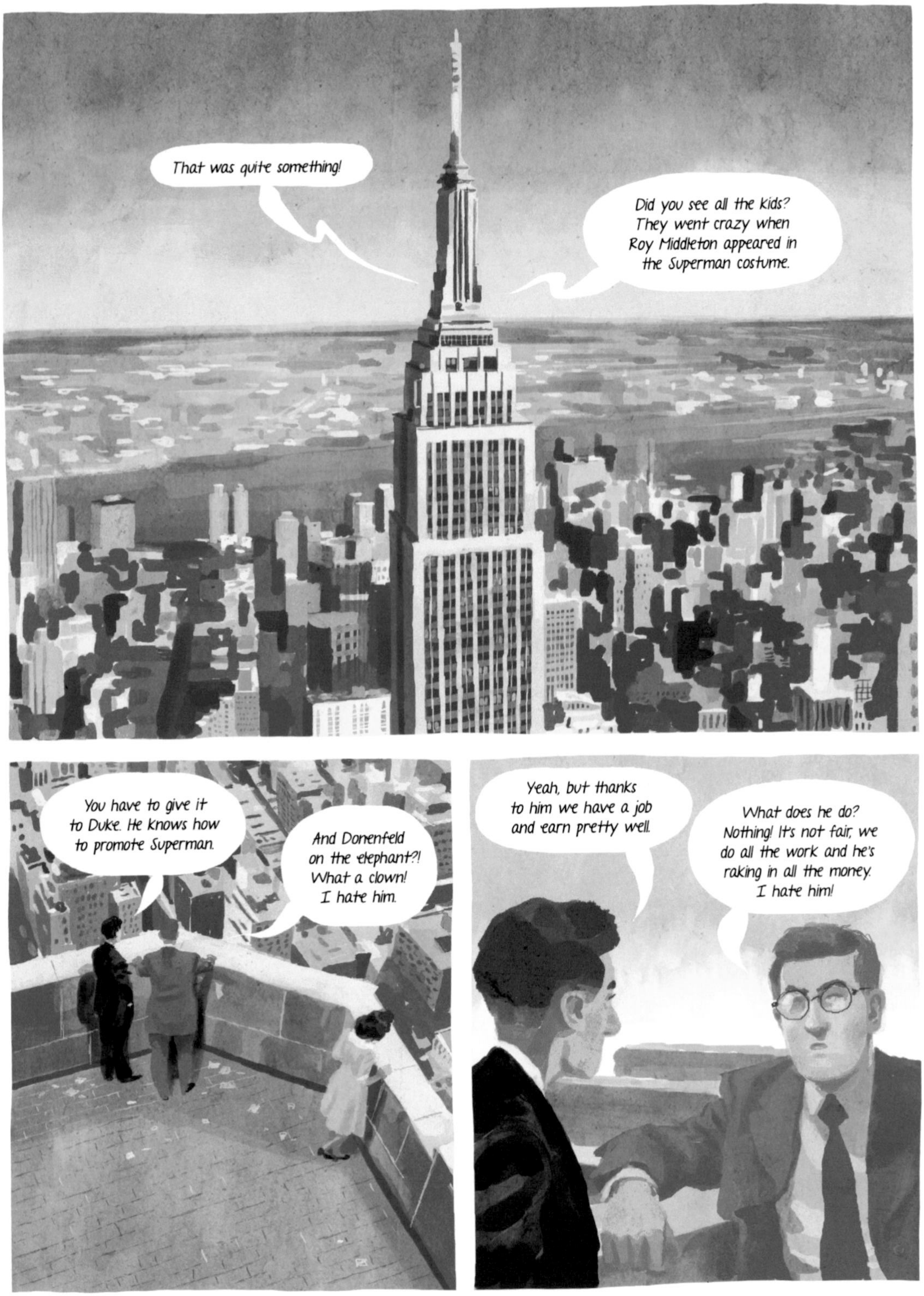
That was quite something!
Did you see all the kids? They went crazy when Roy Middleton appeared in the Superman costume.
You have to give it to Duke. He knows how to promote Superman.
And Donenfeld on the elephant?! What a clown! I hate him.
Yeah, but thanks to him we have a job and earn pretty well.
What does he do? Nothing! It's not fair, we do all the work and he's raking in all the money. I hate him!

Harry, how are you?

Good to see you, boychik! Did you meet Bud Collyer? He's the voice of Superman!

Nice to meet you.

And here is our host, Fred Allen.

Ducovny landed a few other publicity stunts for Superman.

And as much as Jerry disliked Donenfeld, he made good when it came to appearing in public with him.

While Jerry was talking on the Fred Allen Show, I prepared sketches for Dave and Max Fleischer.

They had already created animated films with Popeye and Betty Boop, and now they were bringing Superman to the big screen.

Harry brought me to Miami to see the Fleischer Studios.

I loved the sound effects, the big Technicolor action...

Superman became the most expensive animated short film to date. Paramount spent $50,000 for the each episode! Seeing Superman on the big screen was a dream come true. It was so surreal. Just a few years ago, I was a kid who had to return milk bottles to have enough money to see a movie, and now...

Can we help you?

Oh, no, thank you. I'm looking for my car.

It looks more like you are trying to steal an unlocked car.

What? Oh, no. No, no, no! You see...

What happened, boychik?

I... I couldn't find my car.

Were you drunk?

I was so embarrassed. I had to confess to Donenfeld.

No... it's my eyes.

Your eyes?

I've been having problems with my eyes. I... I first thought it was because of all the work. You know. That my eyes were tired. But...

Come to New York. I know a guy who owes me something. An eye doctor. Good guy. You should see him.

Please, don't tell anyone.

No worries, boychik, no worries.

"My eyesight was one problem, but then my left hand became another. The doctors told me that I had a spastic condition. I could no longer draw for long stretches."

"I switched to the right hand for lettering, and only drew the faces. Everything else was done by the assistants. I spoke to Donenfeld and Liebowitz about it, and they were OK with me just overseeing the work. And so was Jerry."

OK. But you have to pay them from your cut.

"Jerry now only came by the studio to drop off the scripts. I felt that he resented my 'laziness.' I know that he was working very hard, taking on more and more work ."

"He created new features like..."

RED, WHITE and BLUE

"... and "The Star Spangled Kid," the first adolescent superhero with an adult sidekick ."

These features were typical for the zeitgeist. In Europe, after the Nazis and the Soviets had made their non-aggression pact, Germany had invaded Poland. World War II started.

There were stories of pogroms against Jews so gruesome that they were hard to believe. Everybody felt that it was just a question of time until the U.S. would enter the war.

After the German invasion, the editor of Look Magazine asked us to create a Superman story related to the war. Donenfeld loved the idea, Liebowitz was more skeptical.

We created a funny piece in which Superman captures Hitler and Stalin and drops them off at the League of Nations in Geneva.

WHI TAKING US?

GENEVA SWITZERLAND

We did not take it that seriously, but apparently, the Germans did.

See, Jerry, you are now the most hated Yid in Germany!

Harry loved it. And so did Jerry.

Don't worry, Jerry, Superman has your back!

They laughed about the anger, but then the German American Bund started threatening us.

Death to the Jews!

The Bund was an American Nazi organization. The year before, they had held a large rally in Madison Square Garden, demonstrating their support for Nazi Germany.

Have you seen this?

That is awesome.

I heard that Joe Simon and Jack Kirby cut an amazing deal with Timely. Captain America premieres with his own magazine, they have salaried positions and get a percentage of the sales!

Good for them.

Yes. Good for them.

Jerry was haunted by the idea that Donenfeld and Liebowitz were ripping us off.

Do you know how much Donenfeld makes a year?

I dunno.

I spoke with a reporter. He claims that Donny makes over half a million.

O.K.

No, it's not O.K.! We are doing all the work, and make not even a quarter of what he's making. Harry can't write, edit, or draw! Why is he making all the money?

I dunno.

Superman was my brainchild. I came up with the concept. I was the one who started this whole superhero business!

I don't disagree with you. But what'cha gonna do? At least we're getting paid on time. And we are getting paid well.

We are not getting paid well!

112

In early 1941, a second editor was hired to work under Whitney Ellsworth: Mort Weisinger.

Jerry was at first excited that we would be working with Mort. They knew each other from their science fiction fanzines times.

But Mort made it clear that he was in charge, not Jerry.

You might have started it, but you don't have the right to mess it up. There are many people depending on Superman!

Mort forced Jerry to agree to let other writers work on Superman.

I didn't interact much with the editors. I preferred hanging with the other cartoonists, especially Jerry Robinson and Mort Meskin.

Who is this?

Oh, that's Herbie.

That's when I learned who we were actually working for.

Harry Donenfeld's family owned a printing company on the Lower East Side.

Donenfeld was less interested in the printing business, and more in making money.

During the Prohibition, he used the family's delivery trucks not only to transport magazines and newspapers, but also Canadian liquor across the border. That's how he became friends with mobsters such as Waxey Gordon and Frank Castello.

After Prohibition, he started to publish pornography.

When New York Mayor Fiorello LaGuardia started to crack down on public indecency, Donenfeld was indicted for publishing obscene material. The DA was talking about jail time. So Donenfeld needed somebody to take the fall for him.

Herbert, my friend. I have a business proposal for you.

For me?

GIRLS! GIRLS!

SEXY GIRLS   SEXY GIRLS   NEW GIRLS WEEK

Herbie would swear that he was the editor and that he arranged the frontal nudity on the cover, and that he did this without the knowledge of poor, innocent Harry Donenfeld.

Herbie served 90 days in prison and got a job for life.

Donenfeld's company printed for whoever paid. Jack Liebowitz's stepfather was a union organizer for the International Ladies' Garment Workers Union. Donenfeld printed their brochures.

Harry, don't you have a job for my son?

Sure, we'll figure something out.

That's how Liebowitz got the job as Harry's accountant.

After the pornography trial, Liebowitz understood that he had to find a new product for Donenfeld's printing business. That's how they got into comics and how they started to work with the Major.

But this business made them rich, and unlike previous ventures, it was 100% legit.

Superman was their cash cow, and Liebowitz did everything to protect it.

Unless we want a coming generation even more ferocious than the present one, parents and teachers throughout America must band together to break the 'comic magazine.'

When Sterling North, literary editor of the Chicago Daily News, attacked the comic book industry, Liebowitz launched an immediate counterstrike, hiring an 'Editorial Advisory Board' of experts who would speak well of comics.

And when Captain Marvel dared to become the most popular superhero character, even outselling Superman, he hired Louis Nizer, a brilliant copyright lawyer, to work with Superman editor Jack Schiff on destroying Captain Marvel.

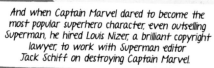

Go get'em, Jack!

Kirby and Simon! How are you guys?

What's happening, Schiff?

We're suing Fawcett. I'm on my way to the lawyer's office. Been spending more time there lately than in my office.

Why are you people suing Fawcett?

They're suing everybody.

Captain Marvel. He's a copy of Superman.

So are a dozen others.

Yes, but Captain Marvel is getting too big. Fawcett's too big. Liebowitz wants to make a test case of Captain Marvel.

Hey, you guys did the first Captain Marvel one-shot. Louis Nizer, our lawyer, should talk to you.

'Bout what?

Didn't they ask you to copy Superman?

That's the point. We can always subpoena you.

Not exactly. Lissen, everybody copied Superman more or less.

Captain Marvel's alter ego was Billy Batson, a kid who could transform himself into an adult superhero by saying the word 'Shazam!'

Captain Marvel's success had to do with the fact that he was in real life a kid, and the kids reading the comic could identify with him. Jerry suggested a new feature, Superboy, focusing on Clark Kent's youth in Smallville, it was rejected by National.

The lawsuit lasted nearly a decade. In the end, Fawcett paid a fine and agreed to retire Captain Marvel.

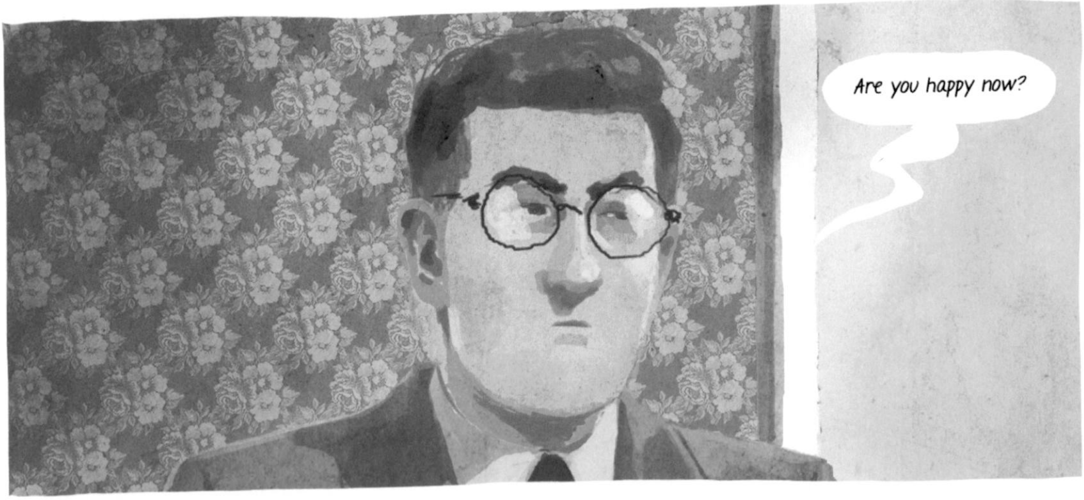
Are you happy now?

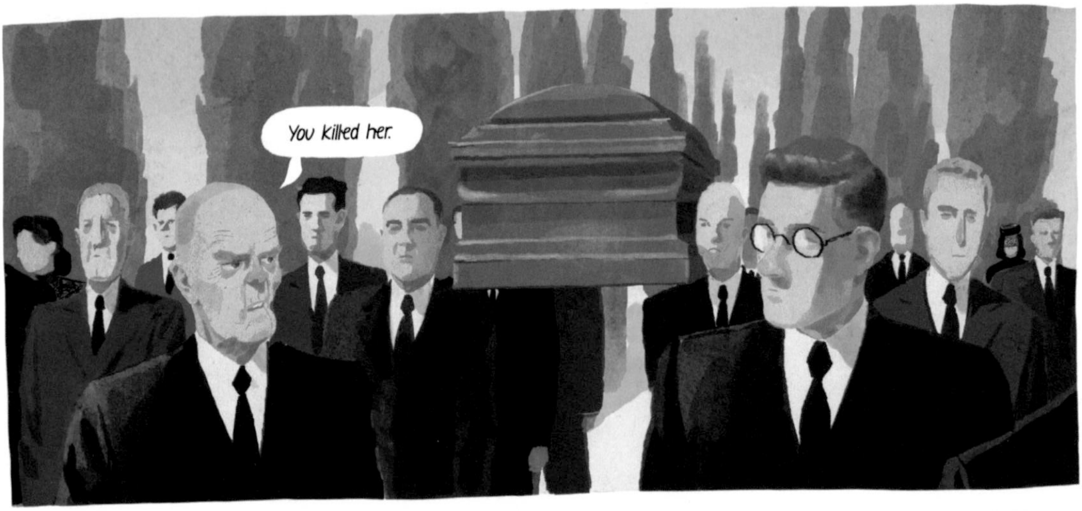
You killed her.

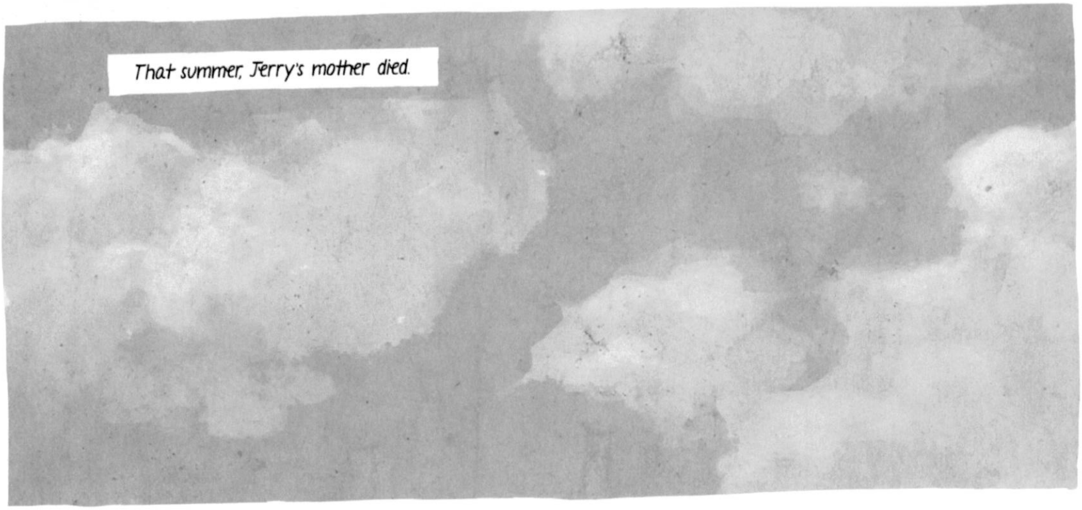
That summer, Jerry's mother died.

Mazal tov!

In December, I was in Toronto attending my cousin's wedding when I learned that Japan attacked Pearl Harbor and the U.S. entered the war.

Other comic book makers send their patriotic-looking heroes into the war to fight Hitler. But not Superman. Jack Liebowitz insisted on keeping Superman out of the war.

MARKS THE SPOT!

KEEP'EM FIRING

The creator of Superman should not have to join the army!

I agree, but what do you want me to do?

But he could not keep Jerry out of the war.

Jerry was drafted; I wasn't because of my eyesight.

On July 4, 1943, during the Festival of Freedom, he was sworn in as the guest of honor. Bob Hope was there, radio personality Wayne Mack was the announcer.

It was a silent goodbye.

Jerry was shipped off to Hawaii, at least not to Europe.

Since Jerry was no longer in Cleveland, National insisted that I'd move the studio to New York. Now that all the other people working on Superman were there, I felt I couldn't say no.

So I moved, but not only the studio. I bought a house in Forest Hills and moved my whole family to New York.

I was earning well, even if I had to spend nearly half my income to pay the other illustrators. I was now in charge. It felt good to be the provider.

Who's this lovely young lady?

That's my sister Jean. Jean, this is Bob...

Bob Kane, the creator of Batman!

Nice to meet you.

How does it feel to be out and about with Batman and Superman?

Wait a minute! Is that Lucille Ball over there?

Yes, and that's Milton Berle.

And living in New York was exciting.

I went on a few double dates with Jerry Robinson. Once, he tried to fix me up with his cousin from Trenton.

So, how'd you like my cousin Shirley?

Oh, well, she's great. But...

But what?

Well, she's too short for me.

You're funny, Shuster. You're funny.

While Jerry was stationed in Hawaii, Bella gave birth to a boy. They decided to name him Michael, after Jerry's father.

I came to Cleveland for the bris. Jerry was telling me all about Honolulu. It sounded exotic and strange to say so even fun.

Jerry's main task was to write for some military publications: Stars and Stripes, Midpacifican, and Yank.

And now I'm a father! My little Superboy!

Jerry was not the only one bringing a "Superboy" to the world. I was shocked when out of the blue I was assigned to do a a new feature: Superboy.

Mister Liebowitz, I just saw the new assignment.

And?

Isn't this Jerry's idea?

But--

Do you have a problem with the assignment?

Yes?

No, no problem.

O.K., is that all?

Yes.

I finished the job and tried to get a copy to send to Jerry, but they would not give me one. So I wrote to him, telling him about 'Superboy.' This feature, I knew, was one of his original ideas.

JACK LIEBOWITZ

Not only did Jerry first suggest Superboy in 1938, and get rejected, but Jerry being Jerry didn't give up and tried again in 1940. And again 'Superboy' was rejected.

But now that he was away, Donenfeld and Liebowitz just went ahead and published Superboy. The first part of the script was Jerry's idea, no doubt, but then the story changed its tone. National had asked Don Cameron to re-write the script.

GREEN ARROW!

TEN CENTS

Superboy was published in 'More Fun Comics' #101.

FUN COMICS

GREEN ARROW! JOHNNY QUICK! DOVER AND CLOVER! AQUAMAN! SPECTRE!

As soon as Jerry got home tensions erupted.

They went ahead without telling or paying me! And you just went along and did it?

What should I have done?

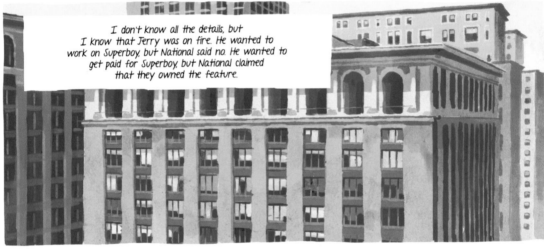

I don't know all the details, but I know that Jerry was on fire. He wanted to work on Superboy, but National said no. He wanted to get paid for Superboy, but National claimed that they owned the feature.

The war in Europe ended and Jerry's war in New York started.

And then the checks got smaller.

The sales are down, Jerry. Here, if you are such a good accountant, then check the books. Superman and Action Comics sales dropped 20%. The times are changing. Kids want Roy Rogers on their pajamas, not Superman.

126

After World War II, superhero sales began to drop. Publishers now turned to humor, western, romance, and especially crime and horror comics.

America was obsessed with crime stories and one of the biggest hits on the newsstand was 'Crime Does Not Pay,' which was soon outselling Superman.

America was changing. The House Un-American Activities Committee was created to investigate alleged disloyalty and subversive activities. As soon as the war ended, the committee's witch hunt started.

Lev Gleason, the publisher of "Crime Does Not Pay," was also one of 16 publishers accused of distributing pro-Soviet propaganda. The case was eventually dropped, but it was a warning for other publishers. Liebowitz was nervous because of his old socialist ties.

The driving force behind the Committee was the Honorable John Rankin of Mississippi, a creep who was convinced that World War II had been produced by an 'international Jewish plot and who infamously called reporter Walter Winchell...

...a little slime-mongering kike.

The committee was going after left-wing publishers and moviemakers, and many of them were Jewish. They also pushed for the U.S. Postal Service to deny second-class mailing rights to any foreign language newspaper that didn't provide a full English translation — the gesture was an obvious slap against the very large Yiddish press.

Yes, America was changing.

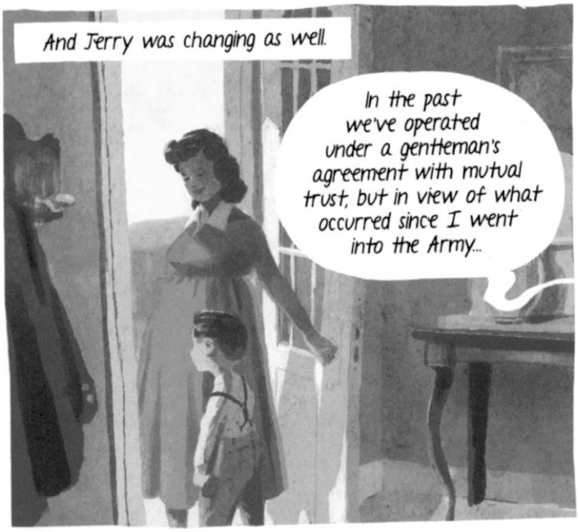
And Jerry was changing as well.
In the past we've operated under a gentleman's agreement with mutual trust, but in view of what occurred since I went into the Army...

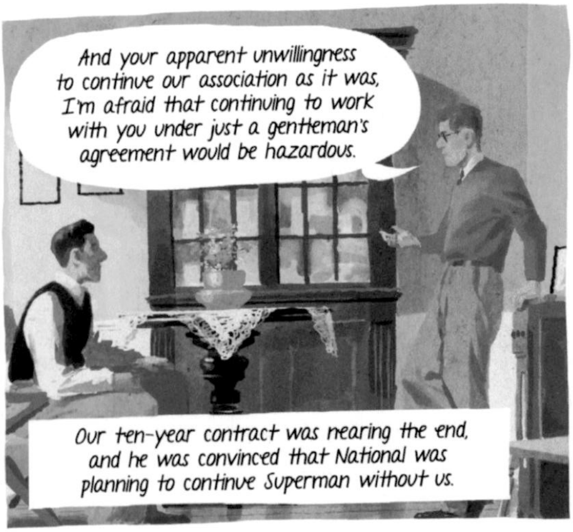
And your apparent unwillingness to continue our association as it was, I'm afraid that continuing to work with you under just a gentleman's agreement would be hazardous.
Our ten-year contract was nearing the end, and he was convinced that National was planning to continue Superman without us.

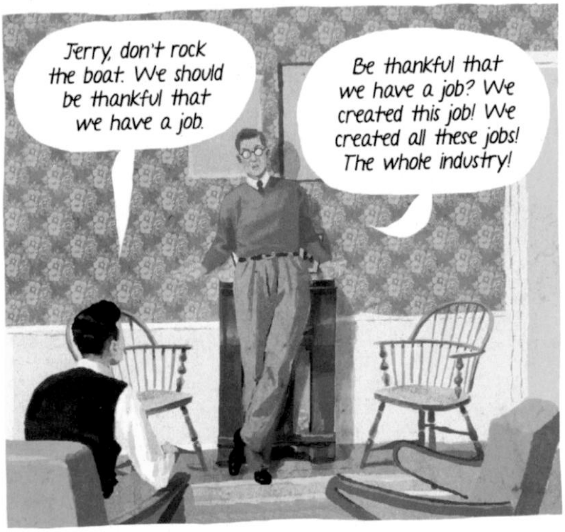
Jerry, don't rock the boat. We should be thankful that we have a job.
Be thankful that we have a job? We created this job! We created all these jobs! The whole industry!

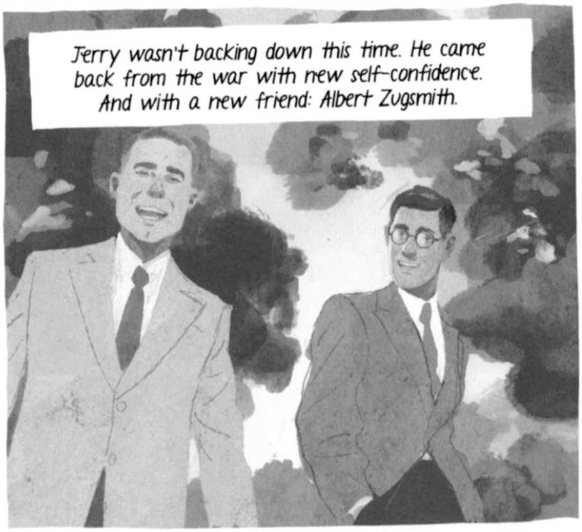
Jerry wasn't backing down this time. He came back from the war with new self-confidence. And with a new friend: Albert Zugsmith.

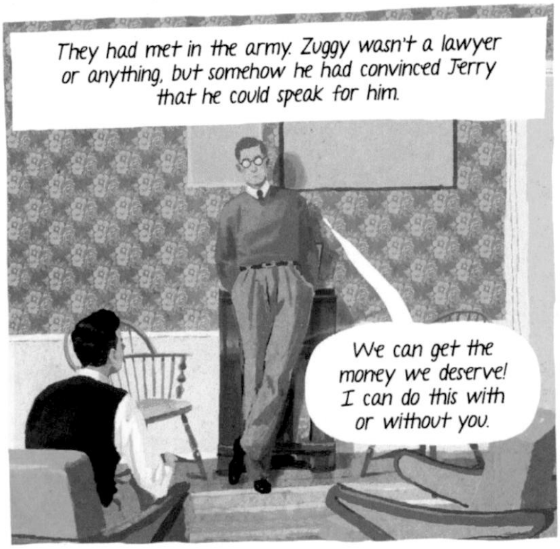
They had met in the army. Zuggy wasn't a lawyer or anything, but somehow he had convinced Jerry that he could speak for him.
We can get the money we deserve! I can do this with or without you.

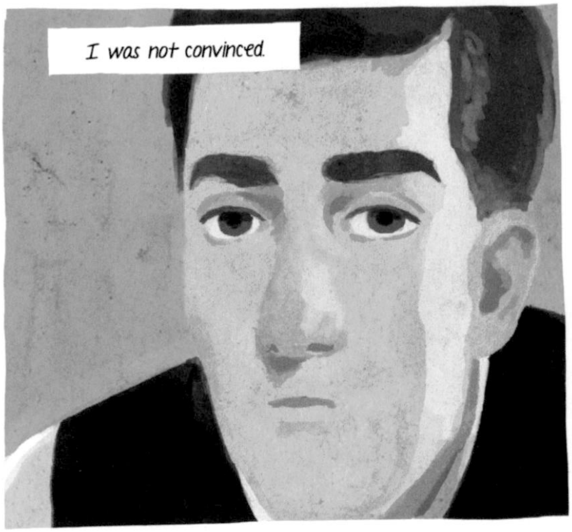
I was not convinced.

But then...

November 1946.

Bella went into labor a month earlier than expected. The boy lived only eight hours. Somehow the cord had gotten around his throat and cut off his air supply.

Jerry was my friend, and I trusted him. So I agreed to join him in his lawsuit.

The first thing we did: We sought allies.

We approached M.C. Gaines who was immediately on our side. Gaines was eager to believe the worst of Donenfeld and Liebowitz.

As a thank you for bringing him *Superman*, Donenfeld had helped Gaines to establish 'All American Comics' with one condition: Gaines had to take on Jack Liebowitz as a partner. It was Donenfeld's way of keeping Liebowitz happy and Gaines under control.

But then the relationship waned, and Donenfeld bought Gaines out so that he could merge National and All-American into one single company. Gaines used the proceeds of the sale to establish Educational Comics focusing on titles such as 'Picture Stories from the Bible' and 'Picture Stories from American History.'

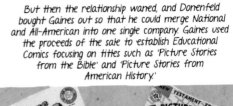

The venture failed. Educational Comics was $100,000 in debt.

I am willing to testify against these crooks.

We then met with Bob Kane. We were hoping he would also sue for his rights for Batman.

We need a united front against them.

Let me think about it.

They are planning WHAT?!

But Bob then renegotiated his original Batman deal.

The ownership of Superman and Batman is indisputable.

But don't you know that your income off Batman is based on an invalid contract?

You signed it.

Sure, but I was a minor at that time.

It was a bluff, but facing a potential mess, Jack agreed to renegotiate a contract with Kane.

Jerry, it's Bob Kane. I've been thinking and I am sorry to say so, but I won't be joining you in your lawsuit.

You're making money without having to work. What's your problem? Seriously, you boys have to grow up.

I have news for you: Nobody cares who writes the stories. Nobody cares who draws the stories. What the kids care about is that it is Superman. We can replace you easily.

Sure, you came up with the comncept, but we published Superman. We made him big.

They first were very patronizing. They didn't take our lawsuit seriously. But when it became clear that we were serious about going ahead with it, they became furious.

I would be interested, just for the record, in having you name one feature -- other than Superman -- out of the numerous ones you've developed, which has enjoyed even a modicum of success.

In April 1947, we sued National for $5 million for the rights of Superman and Superboy. After a couple of lawyers visited Gaines, he no longer supported us.

As soon as we filed, we were out of a job. But we had planned ahead.

Funnyman!

Jerry had approached Jack with the idea for this feature, but it was rejected.

WHEN WE DECIDED TO SUE NATIONAL, WE HAD APPROACHED OUR FORMER EDITOR VIN SULLIVAN, WHO AGREED TO PUBLISH FUNNYMAN AT HIS NEW COMPANY, MAGAZINE ENTERPRISES.

FUNNYMAN WAS THE STORY OF A COMEDIAN NAMED LARRY DAVIS WHO PERFORMS SUPERHERO STUNTS TO OBTAIN PUBLICITY AND WHO FINDS HIMSELF IN REAL CRIME SCENES. IT WAS A SARCASTIC APPROACH TO THE GENRE, SOMETHING TOTALLY NEW.

But it flopped and only ran for six issues.

The following months were nerve-wracking. People were avoiding us.

I don't blame them.

In the end, it all came down to this:
We had sold Superman, but not Superboy.

Zuggy brokered an agreement with National.

O.K., Jack, what will you give me to end this nuisance right now?

What?

Lissen, I want to become a film producer. I need money to start my business.

In the end, National offered us $100,000. We accepted. We had no choice. We needed the money. Debts were piling up. National's lawyers were way superior to ours.

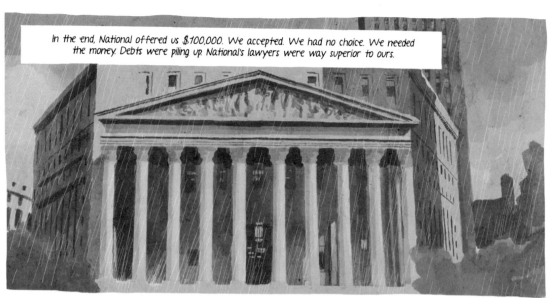

National sent us our last paycheck, then we were fired.

Superman was now officially 'separated' from us.

In 1948, the first live-action Superman movie serial was released.

The idea for this project dated back to 1941. That year, Republic Pictures released 'The Adventures of Captain Marvel,' a twelve-chapter film serial with Tom Tyler in the title role. It was one of the first movie-serials ever made and became hugely popular.

That's when Liebowitz and Donenfeld decided to sue Fawcett and get rid of Captain Marvel.

Kirk Alyn played Superman. Jerry and I both watched it. It was a strange experience.

There was our creation, and it was no longer ours. It's hard to put into words.

There were like 12-15 episodes, but I decided not to watch any more episodes after the first one. It hurt too much.

THE END

Such a clown!

Beep-Beep

Anything happened yet?

No, sir, he hasn't shown up yet.

This isn't good for comics.

Damn inconsiderate of him, pulling this stunt when it's time to go home.

This is no time for sarcasm. It's going to cost all of us.

It's the rush hour, buddy. You're blocking traffic.

I wanna see him jump

You want to see who jump?

Superman. He's going to kill himself... and the whole damn comic book industry.

It was a grey Tuesday in February. A month after the first episode of Superman premiered, Jerry had spread the rumor that he was going to jump off the roof of Grand Central Terminal, killing Superman once and forever.

But he never showed.

On April Fools Day 1948, the Cartoonist Ball was held at the Waldorf Astoria.

Initially I didn't want to go. Everybody knew about us. Everybody knew that we had lost our creation and our jobs. And Funnyman was failing painfully. I don't think it was bad, but it was not Superman. I dreaded the idea of going to the ball and having to face people. But then...

Jolan came to New York. She now called herself Joanne Carter.

She had lived for a while in Chicago, then in Boston.

What shall I go as? Lois Lane? OK., sorry, that was insensitive. How about Dixie Dugan?

In Boston, she had joined a guy in a skating act.

I told him that I couldn't skate, but he said he'll teach me. Unfortunately, the act broke up before we could perform.

She was divorced and now ready to move on.

I'm not sure what I was thinking? All these years we had stayed in touch. I thought it was a good idea to take her to the ball. Jerry would be there as well.

138

He and Bella had issues. Things were not going well and got worse. Jerry now spent more time in New York than in Cleveland.

I was living in Forest Hills with my parents and younger siblings. I felt being the oldest; I had to be the provider for the family. But how could I? I lost my job. And now my eyesight was getting worse. Maybe it was just the stress.

I was worried, very worried.

There we were again. The three of us. We all had our bad experiences, but now, suddenly, we were young again. Life was full of hope.

You're too funny, Jerry.

Ah... of course she is.

Isn't she beautiful, Joe?

Stop it, guys!

Yes, maybe I was still in love with her.

I took her to the ball... but then... I went home alone.

In July, Bella filed for divorce. In October, Jerry and Joanne got married. I did not only lose Superman that year...

On May 14, as the British mandate over Palestine was about to end, the Independence of the State of Israel was declared. Months of war followed. But the Jews won.

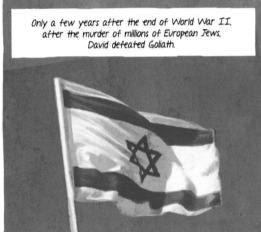

Only a few years after the end of World War II, after the murder of millions of European Jews, David defeated Goliath.

We won, Father.

My father died that year of lung cancer.

In 1951, Julius and Ethel Rosenberg were convicted of espionage for the Soviet Union. They would become the only two American civilians to be executed for espionage-related activity during the Cold War.

The conviction helped to fuel Senator Joseph McCarthy's investigations into anti-American activities by U.S. citizens.

Around that time, it was announced that Kellogg's would sponsor a Superman TV series. Our creation would now conquer yet another new medium: television. Jerry was furious. He wanted to stop this.

Jerry wrote a letter to J. Edgar Hoover.

I often wonder why, in your anti-lurid comics articles and discussions, you never touched on the background of the publishers who manufacture comics trash for profit. What sort of publications did these publishers publish before getting on the comic gravy train?

...ics articles and discussions, you never touched on the background of the publishers who manufacture comics trash for profit. What sort of publications did these publishers publish before getting on the comic gravy trai... Do any of them have criminal or communist records? Did any of them specialize in publishing lewd magazines with titles like 'Hot Stories' and 'Paris Nights' before venturing into the green pastures of the comics field?

I thought you might be interested in having these questions raised by an ex-member of the inner comic fold."

Does anyone know who this Jerome Siegel is?

141

Adventures of Superman' premiered in 1952. George Reeves was playing Superman.

It's OK. You can leave it on.

I heard rumors that Jerry went on a hunger strike, and that National was sending him checks to keep him quiet so that he wouldn't create negative publicity. I don't know if that was true or not. We were no longer in touch.

I was still in Queens, living with my brother who was doing TV rating charts for Nielsen. My sister was now living in Miami, doing a one-woman comedy show.

And I was struggling.

Eventually I got a job.

I got the notes in the mail, did the work, and then took the subway into the city. The address was near Times Square.

I didn't tell anybody about this.

These look great, take the money, my friend, you earned it.

You are not my friend.

I'll soon get more work for you. I'll be in touch.

I felt ashamed.

I knew that what I did was horrible. 'Nights of Horror' was awful, but the publisher paid in full, in cash, and well, what else could I do?

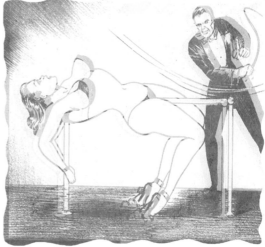

143

You are a parasite to society.

Then, in the summer of 1954, came the Brooklyn Thrill Killers.

The Thrill Killers were a group of teenagers who attacked random victims, tortured and eventually murdered them.

Their leader was dubbed by the media the Boy Hitler of Flatbush Avenue.

The big question was why four normal teens from Brooklyn would commit these horrible crimes?

It came out that they had read 'Nights of Horror.'

I was terrified that someone would find out about my illustrations.

I should have never agreed to do this! Why did I do this? I'll end up in jail. How could I have agreed to do this?

I heard Eddie Mushkin, the publisher, went to prison. I was afraid that someone would link me to him. But the connection was never made.

Frederic Wertham, a psychiatrist, however, made another connection.

All the horrible details are to be found in most of the comic books. I wish to emphatically point out that such crimes did not exist before the comic book era.

CRIME SuspenStories

In his book 'Seduction of the Innocent' he claimed that comic books were dangerous for children.

The number of good comics is not worth discussing, but the great number that masquerade as good certainly deserve close scrutiny. Time has come to legislate these books off the newsstands and out of the candy stores!

If I were asked to express in a single sentence what has happened mentally to many American children during the last decade I would know no better formula than to say that they were conquered by Superman.

Wertham helped spark a Congressional inquiry into the comic book industry.

Superman (with the big S on his uniform-- we should, I suppose, be thankful that it is not an S.S.) needs an endless stream of ever new submen, criminals and "foreign-looking" people not only to justify his existence but even to make it possible. It is this feature that engenders in children either one or the other of two attitudes: either they fantasize themselves as supermen, with the attendant prejudices against the submen, or it makes them submissive and receptive to the blandishments of strong men who will solve all their social problems for them... by force.

The Senate Subcommittee on Juvenile Delinquency was led by Senator Estes Kefauver. In 1950, Kefauver had headed a U.S. Senate committee investigating organized crime that included Donenfeld's old pal Frank Costello. Kefauver embarrassed Costello publicly.

Now he was investigating the comic book industry.

In comic books, life is worth nothing. There is no dignity of a human being.

Wertham called for national legislation that would prohibit the circulation and display of comic books to children under the age of fifteen.

One of the witnesses called to the hearing was Bill Gaines, the son of M.C. Gaines.

His father had died in a boating accident back in '47. When Bill took over his father's company, Educational Comics, was in debt.

My father saw in the comic book a vast field of visual education.

Bill decided to re-launch EC; Educational Comics became Entertaining Comics, and instead of stories from the Bible or American history, he focused on horror and crime.

Here is your May 22 issue. This seems to be a man with a bloody ax holding a woman's head up which has been severed from her body. Do you think that is in good taste?

Yes, sir, I do... for the cover of a horror comic.

The media depicted Gaines as America's most amoral publisher. Within a year, EC was driven out of business. He discontinued all but one venture, EC's last profitable title: 'Mad.'

The Comics Magazine Association was formed to create the Comics Code Authority. John Goldwater of Archie Comics became the president, Jack Liebowitz, the vice president.

Gaines refused to accept the code. Together with his editor Harvey Kurtzman, he converted 'Mad' into a magazine and thus escaped the restrictions of the Comics Code.

If comic books, as the industry claim, are the folklore of today, then the codes are the fables. The problem is really simple. You either close down a house of prostitution or you leave it open.

The comic-book publishers, racketeers of the spirit, have corrupted children in the past, they are corrupting them right now, and they will continue to corrupt them unless we legally prevent it.

The battle was over. But so was most of the comic book industry.

My eyesight got worse and I stopped drawing all together. I found a job as a delivery man, which was OK. I was probably the oldest messenger boy in all of New York City.

Joe? Joe Shuster, is that you?

One day, I had to deliver a parcel to the same building where National was located. I was embarrassed when one of my former colleagues recognized me.

Jack Liebowitz heard that I was in the building and ordered me into his office.

What are you doing here?

I had to deliver a package to the tenth floor.

Close the door, Shuster.

How're you doing?

Look at yourself. That's not a job for you! That's embarrassing. Get yourself together. Here, take $100. And promise me never to come back here. Quit your job. Find something more reasonable.

I did not know it, but Jerry was actually back at National at that time.

DO YOU MIND IF I USE YOUR MANUSCRIPT TO WIPE MY ASS?

"In the late 1950s, Joanne had called National and convinced them to rehire him.

I doubt that Jerry agreed to her calling. Knowing Jerry, he was probably mad she did it. But then again, he was lucky that she did.

This is the most humiliating thing I've ever done.

Liebowitz hired him back on the spot.

It's business; as simple as that.

You will get the standard rate. No extras, no raises, no byline, and you will report to Mort Weisinger.

Jerry's first stories upon returning, even if not credited, appeared in late 1959.

THAT'S SHIT!

Don't worry, Jerry. That's Mort. He does this to everyone.

I know that he likes your scripts.

Thanks, Curt.

Can you get Binder in?

I've got an idea for you, Otto.

Around that time, Jack Liebowitz was trying to take the company public. There was only one problem.

Investor confidence won't be encouraged by the threat of the Justice Department or the SEC investigating us.

So you wanna get rid of me?

It would be better if you resign from the board.

I ain't doing shit! You hear that?!

But then Donenfeld's wife got very ill. He backed off and agreed to resign.

She died in 1961.

It was no secret that Donenfeld had a mistress for decades. And now that his wife was dead, he was finally able to marry her.

Later that year, National made its first public offering with Liebowitz and Sampliner on the board and Donenfeld as a silent partner.

Donenfeld was planning his wedding and honeymoon cruise to Europe.

But then a week before his wedding, he fell and injured his head. When he came out of the ER, he could not speak, he did not recognize his children, and his memory was lost.

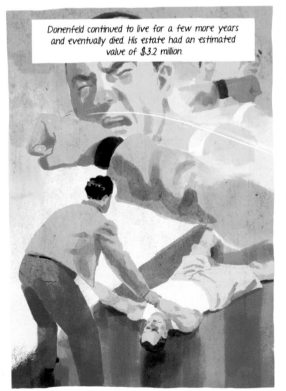

Donenfeld continued to live for a few more years and eventually died. His estate had an estimated value of $3.2 million.

National Periodical Publications did not make an announcement when Harry Donenfeld died.

It's for you, Joe.

In 1963, Jerry contacted me. He was planning to sue National again.

The copyright is up for renewal. We can get Superman back!

I can't. I have no money to pay the lawyers. And honestly, I'm done with this. I don't think we have a chance.

But who was I to stop Jerry?

He had arranged for the attorney to handle the case on contingency basis.

This guy represents motion picture studios in Hollywood, NBC television, he's a top copyright attorney!

COMICS

The moment National got wind of his plans to sue again, he was fired.

So Jerry approached Stan Lee, who, in 1961, had re-launched the old Timely Comics as Marvel Comics. Together with Jack Kirby, Steve Ditko and others, he created a whole new line of iconic superheroes.

MARVEL COMICS

151

Stan gave Jerry a job out of respect, but it did not work out. The times had changed.

The attorney gave us hope. He told us that we would get out of this very wealthy.

The legal claims run out on April 19, 1966. After that date, National will not be able to publish Superman. It's in their interest to settle this.

The trial began in July. There were delays because Liebowitz decided to play hide-and-seek and was reluctant to appear for examination.

A few more months and you guys will be millionaires.

Millionaires! We could only dream.

In January 1966, ABC started to air a Batman TV show. The show made Bob Kane richer than he already was, and Bill Finger even more melancholic.

For decades, Bill was writing for a page rate and remained anonymous. He was the real brain behind Batman, not Bob.

And then there was this guy turning comic book panels into museum pieces.

I think my work is different from comic strips.

Roy Lichtenstein was selling his copies for thousands of dollars, while the artists had sold the originals for $10 or $20 a piece.

The closer my work is to the original, the more threatening and critical the content. However, my work is entirely transformed in that my purpose and perception are entirely different.

Yes, millionaires. We could only dream and wait.

But nothing happened.

The trial hearings went on and on.

We are very, very close.

April 19, 1966 came and went.

But nothing ever happened.

APRIL

19

Tuesday

Jerry left with his family for California. He had finally given up.

I was left alone.

I had a heart attack. The doctors confined me to our home.

I had dizzy spills and a blurred vision.

My mother was now taking care of me. I felt so embarrassed.

I applied to the Social Security Department for disability. It was now clear that we would never get Superman back.

Things got worse every day.

Mother got ill. We used all of our savings to pay for her medical bills.

We were behind in rent and threatened with eviction.

And then mother died right before Thanksgiving 1974.

I decided not to burden my brother anymore. I'd been on the street for a week or so, hadn't eaten in days. And then a policeman picked me up.

THANK YOU FOR THE SOUP.

ONE WAY

DEAD END

EVERYTHING WILL BE ALRIGHT.

A few weeks later...

JOE, THERE IS A LETTER FOR YOU.

And then I got Jerry's letter. Everybody did.

Around that time, it was announced that National Periodical Publications had been paid millions of dollars for the rights to a Superman movie.

So Jerry decided to put a curse on the movie and issued a press release.

YOU'LL BELIEVE A MAN CAN FLY.

ALEXANDER SALKIND PRESENTS MARLON BRANDO · GENE HACKMAN IN A RICHARD DONNER FILM
SUPERMAN

CHRISTOPHER REEVE · NED BEATTY · JACKIE COOPER · GLENN FORD · TREVOR HOWARD · MARGOT KIDDER
VALERIE PERRINE · MARIA SCHELL · TERENCE STAMP · PHYLLIS THAXTER · SUSANNAH YORK
STORY BY MARIO PUZO · SCREENPLAY BY MARIO PUZO, DAVID NEWMAN, LESLIE NEWMAN and ROBERT BENTON
CREATIVE CONSULTANT TOM MANKIEWICZ · DIRECTOR OF PHOTOGRAPHY GEOFFREY UNSWORTH B.S.C.
PRODUCTION DESIGNER JOHN BARRY · MUSIC BY JOHN WILLIAMS · DIRECTED BY RICHARD DONNER
EXECUTIVE PRODUCER ILYA SALKIND · PRODUCED BY PIERRE SPENGLER · PANAVISION® TECHNICOLOR®
AN ALEXANDER AND ILYA SALKIND PRODUCTION

It was more than a press release; it was an essay, a nine-pages long, single-spaced rant about the injustice he and I had suffered.

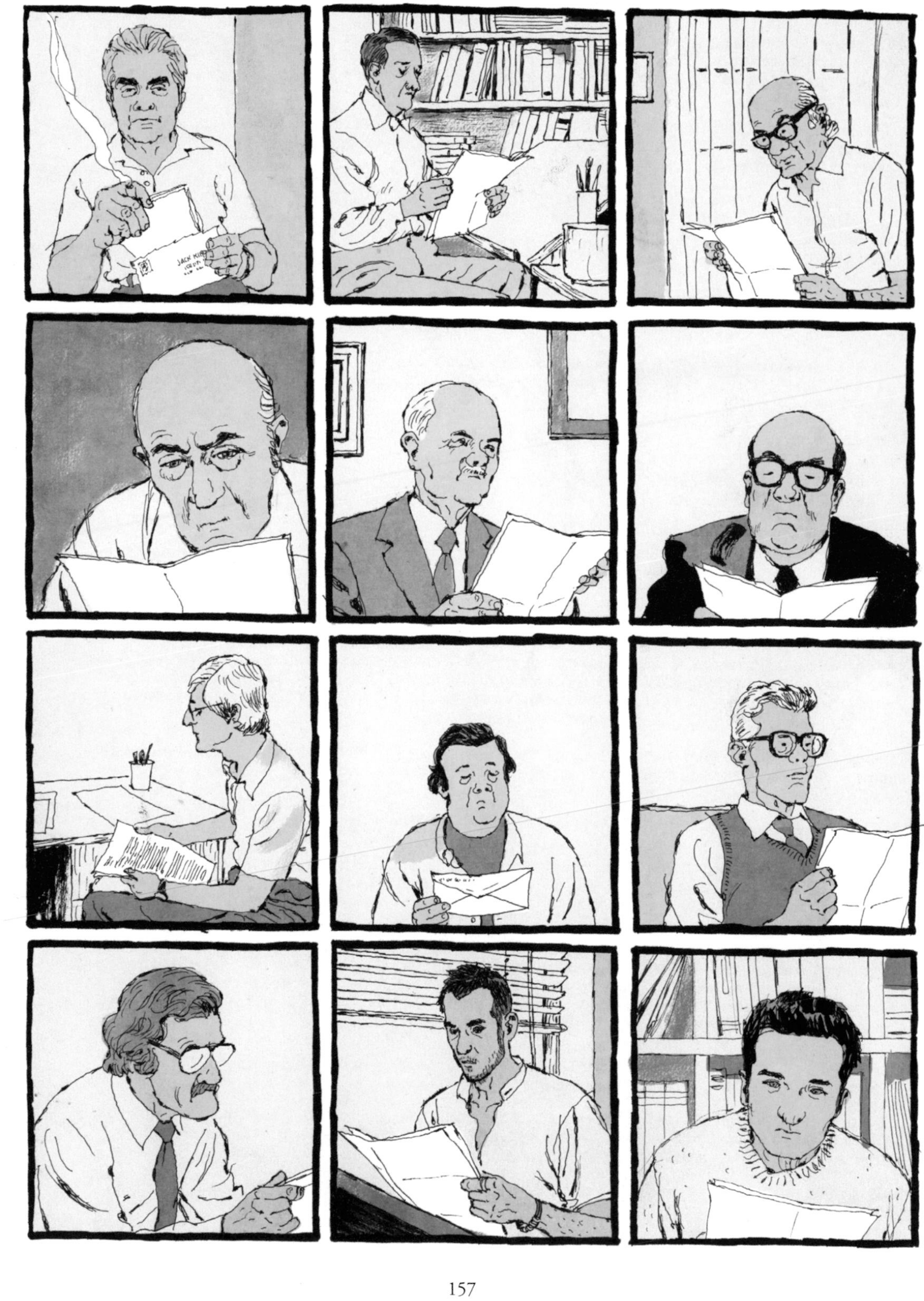

I, Jerry Siegel, the co-originator of Superman, put a curse on the Superman movie! I hope it super-bombs. I hope loyal Superman fans stay away from it in droves. I hope the whole world, becoming aware of the stench that surrounds Superman, will avoid the movie like a plague.

Why am I putting this curse on a movie based on my creation of Superman? Because cartoonist Joe Shuster and I, who co-originated Superman together, will not get one cent from the Superman super-movie deal.

Superman has been a huge money-maker for 37 years. During most of those years, Joe Shuster and I, who originated the character Superman, got nothing from our creation, and through many of those years we have known want, while Superman's publishers became multimillionaires.

The publishers of Superman comic books, National Periodical Publications, Inc., killed my days, murdered my nights, choked my happiness, strangled my career. I consider National's executives economic murderers, money-mad monsters.

Jack Liebowitz stabbed Joe Shuster and me, Jerry Siegel, in the back. He ruined our lives, deliberately, though Joe and I originated Superman, which enriched Liebowitz and his associates.

Liebowitz is extremely wealthy from Superman. But Joe Shuster (the artist) and I (the writer) have received nothing from Superman's phenomenal success most of the 37 years in which our creation Superman has been a great money-maker for National Periodical Publications, Inc.

Joe is partially blind. My health is not good. We are both 61 years old. Most of our lives, during Superman's great success has been spent in want.

Three of the most famous literary creations in publishing history are Tarzan (created by Edgar Rice Burroughs), Sherlock Holmes (created by A. Conan Doyle), and Superman (created by Jerry Siegel and Joe Shuster.)

Edgar Rice Burroughs and his estate profited hugely from TARZAN. A. Conan Doyle and his estate profited hugely from SHERLOCK HOLMES. Yet Joe and I have not only been cheated and ruined by National, but for most of the 37 years of Superman's publication we have received NOTHING from our creation.

The people who cheated Joe and me, as well as their heirs, enjoy the wealth Superman earned and is earning...Superman's current exploiters, including publisher, editors, writers and artists derive big incomes from Superman.

Joe and I suffer...we think of little else, and it makes us miserable to see how our families suffer, too.

So National owns Superman. But what of the two men, Jerry Siegel and Joe Shuster, who originated Superman. Is it right that we get NOTHING from the great success of our Superman creation?

What type of mentality up at National Periodical Publications, Inc. could have done this to us and now permits such an injustice to continue? The ideals which made Superman one of the top comics properties of all time, and caused its creation... namely compassion and a desire to help the oppressed...has been turned into a money-making machine by the organization which callously ruined the lives of Joe and me and deprived us of the fruits of our creation Superman.

The Superman slogan that National has hypocritically cashed in on is "Truth, Justice and the American Way."

The people who exploit and profit from Superman are greedy and selfish. They cheated Joe and me and continue to earn more wealth while Joe and I, the originators of Superman, suffer day after day after day.

Joe and I have been the victims of a monstrous injustice. The double-dealing, the chicanery, the sharp practices and guilt of National are clear.

All Joe and I can do is appeal to someone like you to do whatever you can to aid our cause, and for us to publicize our plight.

The copyright law, which provides for two separate terms of 28 years, was enacted to protect creators, such as Joe and me, from the type of situation we are in.

The creation of Superman, more than any other single event, was responsible for the comic book business as it exists today, creating employment for artists, writers, editors, executives, and others connected with comic book publishing.

Since his first appearance over 37 years ago, our character Superman has been known as a symbol for JUSTICE, the champion of the helpless and oppressed, the physical marvel who had sworn to devote his existence to helping those in need.

We, the creators of Superman, believe it is time for the publishers of Superman to end the great inequity and injustice, which now exists. Joe Shuster and I shall not rest in our present position.

You hear a great deal about The American Dream.

But Superman, who in the comics and films fights for "truth, justice and the American Way," has for Joe and me become An American Nightmare.

What led me into conceiving Superman in the early thirties?

Listening to President Roosevelt's "fireside chats"...being unemployed and worried during the depression and knowing hopelessness and fear. Hearing and reading of the oppression and slaughter of helpless, oppressed Jews in Nazi Germany ...seeing movies depicting the horrors of privation suffered by the downtrodden...reading of gallant, crusading heroes in the pulps, and seeing equally crusading heroes on the screen in feature films and movie serials (often pitted against malevolent, grasping, ruthless madmen) I had the great urge to help...help the despairing masses, somehow.

How could I help them, when I could barely help myself?

Superman was the answer. And Superman, aiding the downtrodden and oppressed, has caught the imagination of a world.

But for most of 37 years the incredible wonder of Superman, his ideals, his accomplishments, have been turned around, like in a ghoulish farce, not only against me, but Joe, too, who had conceived the physical, mystical form of Superman in his artwork.

Superman's publishers have mercilessly gouged Joe and I for their selfish enrichment, stealing our incomes and careers from us derived from Superman, because of their greedy desire to monopolize the fruits of the Superman creation. I can't flex super-human muscles and rip apart the massive buildings in which these greedy people count the immense profits from the misery they have inflicted on Joe and me and our families. I wish I could. But I can write this press release and ask my fellow Americans to please help us by refusing to buy Superman comic books, refusing to patronize the new Superman movie, or watch Superman on TV until this great injustice against Joe and me is remedied by the callous men who pocket the profits from OUR creation. Everyone who has enjoyed our creation Superman and what he stood for, those of you who believe that truth and justice should be the American Way, can help us.

We have been victimized by evil men and a selfish, evil company which callously ruined us and appears to be willing to abandon us in our old age, though our creation Superman has made and continues to make millions for them. Newspaper articles state National was paid $3,000,000 for the rights to make the Superman movie and that $15,000,000 will be spent to produce the movie. And the originators of Superman, Jerry Siegel and Joe Shuster, are not to receive one cent.

We hope the public will never forget this when seeing the Superman character, or National Periodical comic books. Do not patronize Superman because of this injustice.

This might have been the most important piece Jerry ever wrote. Or, let's say the second most important one after the original Superman script.

Among the people who received Jerry's letter was Murray Bishoff, a contributor to the 'Buyer's Guide to Comics Fandom,' a monthly fanzine founded by Alan Light in 1971. The story ran on April 1, 1975.

It might not have been the New York Times, but it had the right readership. Among the people who read the story was Sheldon 'Shel' Dorf. Shel was one of the founders of the San Diego Comic-Con, a comic book convention.

Shel decided to invite Jerry to the Comic-Con.

Finally people wanted to listen to our story.

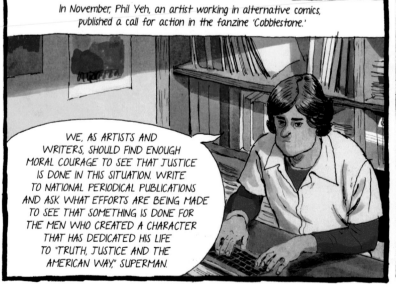

In November, Phil Yeh, an artist working in alternative comics, published a call for action in the fanzine 'Cobblestone.'

WE, AS ARTISTS AND WRITERS, SHOULD FIND ENOUGH MORAL COURAGE TO SEE THAT JUSTICE IS DONE IN THIS SITUATION. WRITE TO NATIONAL PERIODICAL PUBLICATIONS AND ASK WHAT EFFORTS ARE BEING MADE TO SEE THAT SOMETHING IS DONE FOR THE MEN WHO CREATED A CHARACTER THAT HAS DEDICATED HIS LIFE TO "TRUTH, JUSTICE AND THE AMERICAN WAY," SUPERMAN.

And then, slowly, the mainstream media was interested in our story.

NEAL ADAMS SPEAKING. IS THIS JERRY SIEGEL, THE INVENTOR OF SUPERMAN?

YES.

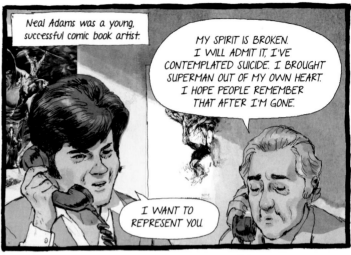

Neal Adams was a young, successful comic book artist.

MY SPIRIT IS BROKEN. I WILL ADMIT IT, I'VE CONTEMPLATED SUICIDE. I BROUGHT SUPERMAN OUT OF MY OWN HEART. I HOPE PEOPLE REMEMBER THAT AFTER I'M GONE.

I WANT TO REPRESENT YOU.

Jerry explained to him that there were no longer any legal options.

NO, NO, I CAN REPRESENT YOU TO THE PEOPLE... I DON'T KNOW WHAT I'LL DO. BUT IF YOU LET ME DO IT, I WILL DO IT. I WILL GET PUBLICITY, I WILL GET ATTENTION, AND I WILL TRY TO TURN THIS AROUND.

And he did.

Neal reached out to Jerry Robinson who was now the President of the National Cartoonists Society.

I WAS UNDER THE IMPRESSION THEY'D REACHED SOME SORT OF SETTLEMENT. I HAD NO IDEA THEY'D STILL BE FIGHTING AND SUFFERING ALL THESE YEARS.

He tracked us down and called us. I hadn't spoken to him in decades.

DRIIIN
DRIIIN

After all those years, people remembered us and spoke up for us.

SIEGEL AND SHUSTER, IN ORDER TO CASH THAT FIRST CHECK FOR $130, WERE OBLIGED TO SIGN A RUBBER-STAMPED CONTRACT ON THE BACK OF THE CHECK, TURNING OVER ALL RIGHTS TO THE PUBLISHER FOR PERPETUITY.

IN EFFECT, SIEGEL AND SHUSTER HAD CREATED A FRANKENSTEIN MONSTER, SINCE THEIR CREATION HAD MADE THE PUBLISHERS MULTI-MILLIONAIRES, ABLE TO HIRE THE BIGGEST LAW FIRMS AND DRAG THE CASE THROUGH THE COURTS UNTIL THE CREATORS HAD EXHAUSTED THEIR MEANS AND, OUT OF DESPERATION, WERE FORCED TO SURRENDER. THEY WERE AWARDED A RELATIVELY MEAGER SETTLEMENT, THEN IMMEDIATELY FIRED.

JERRY AND JOE WERE BOTH GOOD FRIENDS OF MINE. WE WORKED TOGETHER. I WAS DOING BATMAN, THEY WERE DOING SUPERMAN. JOE, THE ARTIST, HAD BAD EYESIGHT EVEN THEN. SINCE THEN HE'S BEEN DECLARED LEGALLY BLIND AND HAS BEEN OUT OF WORK FOR 25 YEARS.

THE WRITER, JERRY SIEGEL, SUFFERED SUCH EMOTIONAL TRAUMA THAT HE COULDN'T CREATE ANOTHER STORY. WE WOULD WALK PAST A NEWSSTAND AND SEE A COPY OF SUPERMAN AND JERRY WOULD GET PHYSICALLY ILL. EVENTUALLY HE SUFFERED A HEART ATTACK AND SETTLED FOR A JOB AS A MAIL CLERK IN CALIFORNIA.

People at Warner Bros. got nervous. Preparations for the Superman movie were made. Lots of money was at stake, and we were bad publicity.

Jerry Robinson and Neal Adams started to negotiate with Jay Emmett, Vice President at Warner Bros., the new owner of DC Comics. We didn't know Emmett, but we knew his uncle, Jack Liebowitz.

In early December, Warner announced that they were willing to settle. But there was one issue left: restoring our byline.

LOOK, JAY. WE'VE GOT TO BRING THIS TO A CLOSE SOMEHOW. YOU WANT THE BAD PUBLICITY TO STOP. GIVE THEM 'CREATED BY' CREDIT AND WARNER LOOKS LIKE THE GOOD GUY.

Friday, December 19, 1975

And then it was done. Our byline was restored, and we were promised a life-long pension.

NOW WE CAN START LIVING AGAIN.

Today, at least, truth, justice, and the American way triumphed.

I am still living in Queens with my brother Frank, but I do no longer want to be a burden to him. Don't get me wrong, I love my brother, but now I know it's time to move on. Jerry tries to convince me to move out West, move to California to be closer to my best friend. And I think I will.

There aren't many people who can honestly say they'll be leaving behind something as important as Superman. But Jerry and I can, and that's a good feeling."

SELECTED BIBLIOGRAPHY

Lauren Agostino and A.L. Newberg, *Holding Kryptonite: Truth, Justice and America's First Superhero,* Holmes & Watson Publishing, 2014.

Thomas Andrae (ed.) and Mel Gordon (ed.), *Siegel and Shuster's Funnyman: The First Jewish Superhero,* Feral House, 2010.

Les Daniels, *Superman: The Complete History,* Chronicle Books, 1998.

Gerard Jones, *Men of Tomorrow: Geeks, Gangsters, and the Birth of the Comic Book,* Basic Books, 2004.

Brad Ricca, *Super Boys: The Amazing Adventures of Jerry Siegel and Joe Shuster – The Creators of Superman,* St. Martin's Press, 2013.

Siegel and Shuster: Dateline 1930's. Previously unpublished work from the creators of Superman. Eclipse Comics, 1984.

Siegel and Shuster, Dateline 1930's #2," Eclipse Comics, 1985.

Joe Simon and Jim Simon, *The Comic Book Makers,* Vanguard Productions, 2003. (Excerpted dialogue from this book is © 2003 by Joe Simon and Jim Simon and is used with permission.)

Larry Tye, *Superman: The High-Flying History of the Man of Steel,* Random House, 2012.

Craig Yoe, *Secret Identity: The Fetish Art of Superman's Co-Creator Joe Shuster,* Abrams ComicArts, 2009.

NOTES

This book is a work of meticulously researched fiction based on the true story of Joe Shuster's life. These notes will quote some of the background material used for its creation and invites the reader to explore more about the history of Superman and his creators. Abbreviated sources are listed in the Selected Bibliography.

Pages 9-11

In 1976, during a symposium at the Mid-American College Art Conference at the University of Nebraska, Jerry Robinson, then-President of the National Cartoonists Society, told the audience about the struggles of Jerry Siegel and Joe Shuster:

"One winter day, Joe was sitting on a bench in the park where he was observed by a policeman to be cold, without a coat, and starving. The officer took him to a luncheonette. He bought him a bowl of soup. A group of kids walked in carrying comic books. Joe noticed that one of the comics was SUPERMAN. Joe said, 'That's my creation – Superman.' The kids looked at him and said he was crazy. The cop said he had just picked him off a bench in Central Park. 'Oh, would you like me to draw a picture?' Joe said. He took out a pencil and drew a picture of Superman on a paper napkin and gave it to the kids. The policeman, perplexed, paid for Joe's soup, then went on his way."

(Quoted in: *The Comic Book Makers*, p. 207.)

The opening scene is based upon this quotation.

Page 11

In the 1960s, in the hope to find employment, Joe printed stationery that identified him as the artist-creator of Superman. In this scene, he sketches on such stationery.

Page 12

The street scene in the first panel is based on a photograph by Roman Vishniac. The Cyrillic letters spell the Russian word for bookstore ("house of books") and the Hebrew letters the Yiddish word for shoemaker, which is "shuster."

Joe's mother Ida Kottiarsky – the spelling of the name varies in historical records – was born around 1890 in a small town in Russia that is known today as Alekseyevka. (Ricca, p. 333)

The word "pogrom" derives from the Russian word for "destroy" and describes a massacre. Its widespread circulation began in the 1880s after a series of anti-Jewish riots in Tsarist Russia. Joe's sister Jean Peavy stated in an interview with Brad Ricca, recorded June 25, 2005, that their mother fled from a pogrom. (Ricca, p. 334)

Page 13

Peavy recalled her mother's journey to Rotterdam in an interview with Ricca. The hotel, located at Wijnburgstraat 8, was owned by Jacob and Roza Shusterowich. (Ricca, p. 11)

According to "Canada Marriages, 1801-1928," Jack Shusterowitz married Bessia on June 30, 1912 and Julius Shusterowich married Ida on September 13, 1913. Their last names were later shortened to Schuster, then Shuster.

Page 14

Joe Shuster was born as Julius Joseph Schuster on July 14, 1914. In Ashkenazi (Eastern European Jewish) tradition, a child is normally not named after a living relative. The fact that Joe carried his father's name, as well as his uncle Jack's (Jacob), the name of his father (Joe's grandfather), underlines that the family was not orthodox. Joe, however, was never known as Julius Jr., but always by his middle name. The birth certificate is part of the Joe Shuster Collection at Case Western Reserve University in Cleveland, Ohio.

Joe had two siblings. His brother Frank (not to be confused with his cousin of the same name) was born four years later, his sister Jeanette ("Jean") six years later.

Joe's cousin Frank would later become half of the famous Canadian comedy team "Wayne and Shuster."

The Schusters's various addresses were identified in the "Toronto City Directory, 1915." (Ricca, p. 12) No sites related to Joe Shuster's life in Toronto are marked, however, there is an uneven street named after him, bordering Dufferin and King Street West. Viewed from above, the three streets form the Superman shield.

Page 15

The movies depicted in this scene are Harold Lloyd's "Safety Last" (1923) and Fritz Lang's "Metropolis" (1927). Joe would later state that "Clark Kent, I suppose, had a little of Harold Lloyd in him." (Quoted in: John Gross, Books of the Times, *Superman at Fifty! The Persistence of a Legend!*, The New York Times, December 15, 1987, accessed online at http://www.nytimes.com/1987/12/15/books/books-of-the-times-193487.html)

Pages 16-17

In his last interview, only a few months before his death, Joe Shuster told Henry Mietkiewicz: "In those days, color comics were published on a large scale. They would devote an entire page to one comic, usually with vivid colors very bright, vivid colors. Of course, I was only 3 or 4 and I couldn't read. So we [my father and I] had a ritual. We would both open up the color comics and my father would read all the dialogue and balloons. I remember the Katzenjammer Kids, Boob McNutt, Happy Hooligan, and Barney Google. But my sharpest memory is of Little Nemo."

(The Toronto Star, April 26, 1992)

Page 18

In an interview with Shel Dorf (March 1984), Joe Shuster recalled his childhood inspirations: "What I considered the best inspiration was seeing the work of artists like Milton Caniff, Alexander Raymond, and well-known science fiction artist Frank R. Paul who did illustrations for Wonder Stories magazine. When I was very young, my favorite comic strip was 'Little Nemo' by Winsor McCay. Fantastic imagination and marvelous detail were there which I've never seen since."

(*Dateline*, p. 16)

Page 19

The Shusters crossed the border at Niagara Falls in August 1924 (Ricca, p. 13). Even though Joe left Canada as a ten-year old, the Canadian Comic Book Creator Awards are named after him.

The Richman Brothers Company was originally founded in 1853 by Henry Richman Sr. and his brother-in-law Joseph Lehman, Jewish immigrants from Bavaria. By the 1930s, Richman Brothers billed itself as "World's Largest Manufacturers of Fine Men's Clothing."

The city of Cleveland increasingly markets its connection to Superman. Here a t-shirt referencing Superman.

Page 21

"My mother wanted me to become a doctor, but I myself never considered anything but the art field, either becoming an artist, illustrator, or cartoonist." Joe Shuster in an interview with Shel Dorf, March 1984. (*Dateline*, p. 16)

Page 22

Brad Ricca uncovered some of Joe Shuster's contributions to The Federalists in his book. (p. 15)

Page 23

"Joe and I went to elementary school together and he was always an amazing artist," Jerry Fine recalled in 2009 at the first meeting of the Siegel and Shuster families in Cleveland. "We did a comic strip together for the newspaper called 'Jerry the Journalist,' where I was depicted as a grasshopper."

(Michael Sangiacomo: "Jerry Fine dies, he brought Superman creators Jerry Siegel and Joe Shuster together," The Plain Dealer, December 29, 2013.)

Page 25

In his book, Larry Tye imagines Jerry Siegel being bullied in school: "Tormentors were everywhere. Some tripped him as he tried to escape, others punched. His very name became a source of ridicule. 'Siegel, seagull, bird of an eagle!' they would chant." (p.4)

Page 26

Both Joe Shuster and Jerry Siegel date their first meeting to 1931, see interview with Shel Dorf. (*Dateline*, p. 14)

Pages 27-28

The Shuster residence is long gone, but in 2009, the not-for-profit Siegel and Shuster Society erected a fence around the site of the former apartment building and also did some much needed repair work on the house of Jerry Siegel. The then-owners, who had purchased the home in 1983, had no idea that they owned a deed to Americana. The streets where Siegel and Shuster lived received honorary names: Kimberly Avenue is today "Jerry Siegel Lane," nearby Parkwood Lane is "Lois Lane," and Armor Avenue, where the Shuster apartment was located, bears the honorary name "Joe Shuster Lane."

(Marc Bona: "Superman's birthplace, in Jerry Siegel's Cleveland home, gets recognition," The Plain Dealer, September 4, 2009.)

Former home of Jerry Siegel. The fence shows the original Superman shield.

Page 28

Julius Shuster lost his job in 1929 and the family was depending on charity for a while before he became an elevator operator at Mount Sinai Hospital. (Ricca, p. 40)

Page 29

Larry Tye used for his book an unpublished memoir, copyrighted by Jerry Siegel in 1978 as *"Creation of a Superhero."* This anecdote, described in Tye's book as follows, is probably based on Siegel's recollection: "He climbed onto the roof of the garage holding an umbrella. 'I opened the umbrella and leaped. Look out world, here I come!... I did this over and over again.'" (Tye, p. 5)

Page 30

The science fiction sketch Jerry holds in his hand was titled "World in Future – 1980." It was reprinted as the cover of *Dateline #2*. According to Jerry Siegel, it was the first piece of Joe's art he ever saw. The original artwork was dated ("May 2, 1931") and the age of the artist ("16 YRS") indicated.

(*Dateline #2*, p. 1)

Hugo Gernsback (nee Gernsbacher, 1884-1967) was an inventor and publisher, who is considered to be one of the "fathers of science fiction" (the annual World

Science Fiction Convention awards are named after him). His contributions to the genre as publisher are often compared to those of novelists such as H.G. Wells and Jules Verne. Gernsback was also a radio pioneer.

Frank Paul (1884-1963) was an American pulp illustrator who was influential in defining the look of Hugo Gernsback's magazines in the 1920s. Paul was known for dramatic compositions, often showcasing robots and spaceships, as well as bright colors. His most famous "Amazing Stories" cover was published in 1927 and is an illustration of H.G. Wells *"War of the Worlds"* (shown in the 4th panel on this page). In 1939, Paul painted the cover of the first issue of MARVEL COMICS, an issue that featured the debut of the Human Torch and the Sub-Mariner.

Page 31

The story Jerry narrates is Edgar Rice Burroughs's *"A Princess of Mars,"* the first part of his Barsoom series. The novel is considered a classic example of 20th century pulp fiction.

Page 32

"Jerry Fine remembered [Jerry Siegel] trying to impress his cousin at one family gathering. 'I can write a story about anything. You see that Coke bottle? I could write a story about that Coke bottle if I wanted to.'" (Jones, p. 77)

Page 34

Bernarr Macfadden (1868-1955) was a proponent of physical culture, combining bodybuilding with nutritional and health theories. In 1899, he founded "Physical Culture," a magazine that started his publishing empire. He was the predecessor of Charles Atlas and is widely considered the person who started fitness culture in the United States.

Page 35

The Cleveland Public Library Digital Gallery has in its collection of high school yearbooks and student newspapers several issues of the Glenville Torch. The story here is based on Jerry Siegel's "Master Sleuth Solves Very Baffling Enigma," published in the Torch in 1931. The murder mystery features "Jerry Siegel, master of deduction," as the detective. (Glenville Torch, Vol. XI, No. 28, May 21, 1931, p.2)

Page 36

The names of Lois Donaldson and Maxine Kent can be found on old mastheads. Is it pure coincidence that there would be later another Lois (Lane) working at a newspaper with a (Clark) Kent?

Page 37

The Glenville Torch, Volume XIV, No. 9, November 29, 1933 features Joe's Thanksgiving cartoon prominently on the front page.

Page 38

The poem was published in the Glenville Torch on December 1, 1932 (Vol. XIII, No. 10) on page two and signed "This looks a lot like Stiletto's work, Miss Amster." – a reference to Jerry's alter ego and the main character of his detective stories published in the paper.

When Lois Amster Rothschild died in 2014, her

obituary mentioned that "Lois's claim to fame is that she attended high school with Jerry Siegel and Joe Shuster, the creators of Superman, and she was the inspiration for the character Lois Lane."

(Michael Sangiacomo: "Lois Amster, one of the inspirations for Superman's Lois Lane, dies at 97," The Plain Dealer, April 29, 2014)

Page 39

In *"Men of Tomorrow,"* Gerard Jones reported that Jerry's father was shot during a robbery, however, since the book was published new sources became available. In three entries to his blog "Noblemania," Marc Tyler Nobleman published the coroner report ("The death of Jerry Sigel's father," September 3, 2008), the police report (September 12, 2008), and a newspaper report (September 17, 2008), all indicating that Mitchell Siegel died of a heart attack.

(www.noblemania.com)

Jerry Siegel and Joe Schuster in their high school yearbook.

Page 40

Jerry Siegel recalls his encounter with his English teacher in an interview with Shel Dorf: "English was the one class I enjoyed immensely. The stuff that I self-published by mimeograph and sold through the mail,

I brought to my English teacher. She had me stay after class and her comment was, 'Why do you write this type of material (science fiction) when there are so many wonderful things you can write about?' I said, 'Well, that's what I like!' She shook her head as if to say, 'there goes another lost soul,' and that was the end of that! Back in those days science fiction was really in the lower depths as far as public acceptance went." (*Dateline*, p. 17)

Pages 41-42

Ricca reprints in his book (p. 62-64) not only the news clippings from the Charity Football Poster contest, but also the poster itself, which is incorporated in the illustrations.

Pages 43-45

Ricca dedicates a whole chapter in his book (Chapter 6: Reign, p. 65-79) to this first Superman story. Images of "The Reign of the Super-Man" can be found all over the internet.

Pages 48-49

Jerry Siegel remembers this encounter as follows: "Joe and I got busy co-creating what we believed was another red hot project: a nationally distributed monthly comics tabloid to help get the country's mind off breadlines and overseas dictators. We called it POPULAR COMICS. [...] Amazingly, we got a contract from The Cleveland Shopping News, which owned a color printing press; one of the company's activities was publishing color comics advertising giveaways for department stores. A contract! Signed! Fame, success, and big money was just around the corner! See, world – see what faith and stick-to-it-iveness can do! [...] Our hopes for the comics tabloid, however, died quickly. The publisher changed his mind and it was never published. [...] The only thing that kept Joe and me from going bonkers was the delicious odor of corned beef wafting seductively from out of Solomon's Delicatessen on Cleveland's East 105th Street. Unfortunately, Joe and I could only inhale the mouthwatering fragrance. We were too broke to swagger in and buy [...] even one sandwich to wolf down between us."

(*Dateline* #2, p. 1)

Pages 50-53

By claiming that the idea for Superman came to him in a dream, Jerry Siegel created the creation-myth of Superman. Jerry re-told this story many times, for

Marker on East 105th Street.

instance in the 1981 BBC documentary "The Comic Strip Hero."

Page 54

Joe Shuster recalls his challenging beginning as an artist, but also his parents being supportive. "Once they saw how serious I was at becoming an artist, my mother and father gave me a lot of support. I had no drawing board at the time, no art supplies. My mother gave me her breadboard to work on when she wasn't using it. Every Friday, she would make the Challah, the bread for the Sabbath. Then she'd take the board away from me. The board was made of wood with little side rails, and I would prop it up on the dining room table and draw." (*Dateline*, p. 17)

"DETECTIVE DAN, SECRET OPERATIVE NO. 48" was published by Chicago-based "Humor Publications." The main character, Dan Dunn was an imitation of Chester Gould's "Dick Tracy."

Page 55

Humor Publications's reply to Jerry Siegel, dated August 23, 1933, as quoted in Daniels. (p. 17)

Page 57

After his falling out with Joe, Jerry contacted several other artists and asked them to draw Superman samples for him. (Ricca, p. 99)

Page 59

Malcolm Wheeler-Nicholson (1890-1965) was the author of nonfiction books about the military before turning to pulps. After having seen the emergence of *"FAMOUS FUNNIES"* and other oversize magazines reprinting comic strips, he formed his own company "National Allied Publications" in 1934. His premiere series "NEW FUN," the first comic book containing all-original material, was published in 1935 (cover date February 1935).

In the fifth panel on this page, The Major is holding wallpaper containing Joe's sample pages. Joe Shuster recalls in an interview with Shel Dorf that, due to the lack of supplies, often recycled paper was used. "When I had no paper, sometimes I would use brown wrapping paper. I remember I once found several rolls of wallpaper. I was overjoyed. The back was white and I had enough drawing paper to supply me for a long time. We submitted two strips to Major Wheeler-Nicholson, 'Henry Duval' and 'Dr. Occult': one was done on brown paper, and one on the back of wallpaper. When it was sold they told us to redraw it and we went out and bought good paper." (*Dateline*, p. 17-18)

Pages 62-69

Joanne Siegel (nee Jolan Kovacs) recalls her first encounter with Jerry and Joe in an interview with Shel Dorf: "Joe had apparently told [Jerry] that he hired a model. When we came out, there was Jerry waiting to meet me. He was the most energetic kid I had seen in my life. He was constantly in motion. [...] We three had an instant rapport. Joe was very shy and quiet. Jerry was very outgoing. Eventually we became the 'three musketeers.' [...] We were all on our school newspaper. I was a feature writer. My ambition was to become a newspaper reporter. [...] But I'll settle for being the model for the most famous girl reporter in the world – Lois Lane." (*Dateline*, p. 33)

Page 72

NEW FUN # 6 was dated October 1935.

Page 78

Major Malcolm Wheeler-Nicholson, letter to Jerry Siegel, October 4, 1935, quoted in Ricca, p. 146.

Jerry's words were a quote in 2009 trial "Joanne Siegel and Laura Siegel Larson vs. Warner Bros. Entertainment," see Ricca, p. 134.

The text in the last panel is from a letter by United Feature Syndicate. (Tye, p. 28)

Pages 79-82

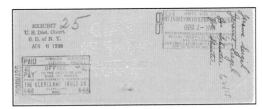

Sheldon Mayer's granddaughter Chelle has a tattoo of her grandfather on her shoulder.

In March 2016, Sheldon Mayer's granddaughter Chelle described to me in an email exchange how Superman got published.

The dinner took place at the home of Jenny and Leo Mayer, Sheldon's parents. Like Jerry and Joe, Sheldon still lived with his parents. Michelle "Chelle" Mayer confirmed the details with her uncle Monroe "Monte" Mayer, Sheldon's younger brother via email: "Leo was a butcher, it was during the Depression, they ate whatever he brought home. At dinner, there was no one else except the four of us, and Jerry & Joe. No clue on the date or what we had, but it was during the throes of the Depression, and Leo was a butcher as was his father, thus, I know it was a meat meal." (March 2016)

Pages 84-85

In 2011, the original check was obtained by Stephen Fishler of ComicConnect.com and Metropolis Comics, companies specializing in rare collectibles, and went viral after Gerry Duggan posted a digital image of this artifact on Twitter on October 23, 2011, see also:

http://comicsalliance.com/superman-check-jerry-siegel-joe-shuster-dc-comics/

Page 86

ACTION COMICS #1 was published in April 1938 and dated June 1938. It is considered the beginning of the superhero genre. In 2014, a pristine copy of the comic sold for over $3 million, making it the most expensive comic book in history.

Vincent Zurzolo with a copy of ACTION COMICS #1. Zurzolo, together with Stephen Fishler, purchased this copy for $3.2 million.

Pages 87-88

The circulation numbers and survey results are quoted in Larry Tye's book (p. 36-37). There have been several reprints of ACTION COMICS #1, including DC's *"The Superman Chronicles"* series (vol. 1 published in 2013).

Page 92

Liebowitz's words are quoted from his letter to Jerry Siegel, dated September 28, 1938.

(Ricca, p. 156)

Page 94

Will Eisner (1917-2005) was one of the pioneers of the American comic book industry. His series "THE SPIRIT" (1940-1952) revolutionized sequential storytelling through his experimental use of content and form. In 1978, he published *"A Contract with God,"* widely considered (yet still hotly debated to be) the first graphic novel. The Eisner Awards are named in his honor. He was one of the three inaugural inductees to the Will Eisner Comic Book Hall of Fame.

The copyright infringement lawsuit against Fox's *"WONDER MAN"* due to the similarities to Superman started on March 15, 1939. It was the first copyright lawsuit in comic book history and set a precedent for National Comics's vigorous protection of its characters.

Page 96

There are different versions of the Batman foundation myth, but they all state that on a Friday Vin Sullivan asked his contributors to bring in a new feature for DETECTIVE COMICS by Monday.

(Jones, p. 149)

Milton "Bill" Finger (1914-1974) was for many years the forgotten co-creator of Batman. Finger also co-created the original Green Lantern. He died impoverished and was posthumously inducted into the Jack Kirby Hall of Fame in 1994. In 1999, Jerry Robinson founded the Bill Finger Award for Excellence in Comic Book Writing, presented annually at the San Diego Comic-Con. In 2006, author and historian Marc Tyler Nobleman started a crusade to credit Finger for his contributions to Batman. His quest is part of the 2017 documentary "Batman and Bill." In 2015, DC Entertainment announced that Finger would be officially acknowledged, in the form of the revised credit line, "Batman created by Bob Kane with Bill Finger," that would now appear in all Batman films, television shows, and comics.

Page 97

Joe Simon explains in "The Comic Book Makers" (p. 54) that these "text stories" in comics were created to satisfy Post Office regulations for second class mailing privileges. Since it was "commonly believed that no one read these two-page text stories" they were given at Timely Publications to Martin Goodman's wife's cousin, Stanley Lieber who was Simon's editorial assistant. Lieber signed his first text story assignment as Stan Lee. Simon recalls the following conversation:

Simon: Who's Stan Lee?

Lee: I'm changing my name. For journalistic reasons.

Simon: It would be better for a laundry.

Lee: I hadn't considered that. I wonder what the comic book prospects are in China.

In 2013, attending Wizard World Comic Con in New York, Stan Lee was asked by author Julian Voloj about his early text stories. The quotation is taken directly from Lee's reply.

Stan Lee at Wizard World

Pages 100-101

According to Larry Tye, Jerry's mother "Sarah had never liked Bella. She knew the bride's mother, who could neither read nor write, and her father, who fixed broken toilets and unclogged sinks for a living. Sarah Siegel came from the same impoverished ghettos of Eastern Europe as Sam and Esther Lifshitz, and had experienced enough hardship in the New World to last two lifetimes. But she was a proud American Jew now – the kind who learned the language and how to get by, and who put on rouge, lipstick, and a hat to go to the grocer because you never knew who you'd run into – and she couldn't abide people like the Lifshitzes who hadn't adjusted." (Larry Tye, p. 47-48)

Page 102

Jerry was known to listen to Benny Goodman while working at home. The song playing is the 1934 "Moonglow" by Goodman.

Pages 102-103

In 1941, the Saturday Evening Post ran a feature on the business of Superman that included photographs of both Siegel and Shuster in their homes.

John Kohler: "Up, Up and Awa-ay! The Rise of Superman, Inc.," Saturday Evening Post, June 21, 1941. A PDF of the feature can be found on the paper's website:

http://www.saturdayeveningpost.com/wp-content/uploads/satevepost/rise-of-superman.pdf

Page 103

"The Adventures of Superman" was one of the longest-running radio serials and aired from February 12, 1940 to March 1, 1951 and had a total of 2088 episodes.

The first 170 episodes can be listened to online at:

https://archive.org/details/superman_otr

Page 104

The 1939-1940 World's Fair in New York took place in Flushing Meadows-Corona Park and was the second most expansive American World's Fair of all time, covering over 1,200 acres. Over 44 million people attended the exhibition. It was the first exposition to be based on the future, inviting visitors to take a look at the world of tomorrow.

Jerry took Bella to the World's Fair for their honeymoon, see Tye, p. 48.

Page 105

There is fascinating footage of the Superman Day event at the World's Fair on YouTube:

https://www.youtube.com/watch?v=dhYzI1J1fNI

The description reads: "Amazing Kodachrome film footage of 'Superman Day' events plus the very first Superman to don the superhero's cape 'Ray Littleton' [sic] taken at the World's Fair in New York way back in 1939. There is even some brief footage of Jerry Siegel the creator of Superman."

Mark Evanier identified on his blog (9/22/2002) the actor who played Superman at the World's Fair as Ray Middleton who "later had a pretty impressive career on Broadway. He was the original Frank Butler in Annie, Get Your Gun, playing opposite Ethel

World's Fair Memorabilia from the permanent exhibition at the Queens Museum

Merman's Annie Oakley, and he can still be heard on the cast recording. He had two roles in the original production of Man of La Mancha and was also in South Pacific, Love Life, and Roberta, to name three of many others. He made a few film appearances, including a role in our favorite, 1776, and did a lot of TV jobs, including a recurring role on Too Close for Comfort. He passed away in 1984."

https://www.newsfromme.com/2002/09/22/the-first-superman/

Page 106

Brad Ricca posted footage from the visit to the Empire State Building onto YouTube on September 24, 2013. From the description by Ricca: "This footage depicts Jerry Siegel in 1940 (with his wife Bella) as they visit New York City and go to the top of the Empire State building. In 1940, Jerry and Superman were on top of the world. It would not last."

https://www.youtube.com/watch?v=HVHrXfdLLWs

Page 107

The audio file of Fred Allen interviewing Jerry – worth a listen just to hear Jerry's squeaky voice – can be found online:

https://www.audiosparx.com/sa/archive/Radio/Radio-introductions-and-interviews/Fred-Allen-Interviews-Superman-Writer-Jerry-Siegel/236269

The Superman cartoons were the character's first animated appearance. Nine cartoons were produced by Fleischer Studios and released in 1941 and 1942 by Paramount Pictures, eight more were produced in 1942 and 1943 by Fleischer Studios's successor. Superman was the final animated series by Fleischer Studios before they were officially taken over by Famous Studios. All seventeen shorts can be found on YouTube: https://www.youtube.com/watch?v=PiuTMnSVRwA

Page 108

In the winter of 1940, Joe was due to go out with a couple of girls in Miami Beach, but never showed. He was stopped on the street near his hotel, ogling an antique car, but due to his myopic vision, he leaned in too close and a patrolmen spotted and arrested him as a would be auto-thief. Harry Donenfeld was in town and had to bail him out. (Tye, p. 53)

Page 109

Joe acknowledged early that he could not handle the workload. His eyes were bad and for a while he had a spastic condition involving his left hand that prevented him from drawing for long stretches. He switched to his right hand for lettering and was forced to wear a brace. Back then, Joe drew the same salary as Jerry, but when he decided to hire assistants – their bylines never appeared– Jerry made it clear that they had to be paid out of his cut. (Tye, p. 52)

Page 110

"How Superman Would Win the War" was published in the February 27, 1940 issue of Look Magazine, accompanied with a one-page introduction about ACTION COMICS, Jerry Siegel and Joe Shuster. The comic and introduction can be found here: http://www.archive.org/stream/HowSupermanWouldEndTheWar/look#page/n1/mode/2up

A copy of Look Magazine with "How Superman Would End the War" found its way to Das Schwarze Korps, the weekly newspaper of the SS (short for "Schutzstaffel," literally "Protection Squadron"), a paramilitary organization under Hitler's Nazi party. The fact that Superman's originators were Jewish provided opportunity for a particularly enthusiastic attack. In the April 25, 1940 issue, page 8, they wrote:

"Jerry Siegel, an intellectually and physically circumcised chap who has his headquarters in New York, is the inventor of a colorful figure with an impressive appearance, a powerful body, and a red swim suit who enjoys the ability to fly through the ether. The inventive Israelite named this pleasant guy with an overdeveloped body and underdeveloped mind 'Superman.' He advertised widely Superman's sense of justice, well-suited for imitation by the American youth. […] Woe to the American youth, who must live in such a poisoned atmosphere and don't even notice the poison they swallow daily."

The best source in English on the Schwarze Korps is William L. Combs, *The Voice of the SS: A History of the*

SS Journal *"Das Schwarze Korps"* (New York: Peter Lang, 1986).

The above quoted text was posted online in 1998 by Randall Bytwerk on Calvin College's German Propaganda Archive: http://research.calvin.edu/german-propaganda-archive/superman.htm

Tye mentions in his book that the German American Bund did sent hate mail to Joe in the years leading up to the war and that some of their members picketed outside the National Comics headquarters (p. 78).

Jones reports that Harry Donenfeld, always ready for a good laugh, enjoyed when his friends greeted him with "Hey, Superman!" He would strike a pose and yell the slogan from the Superman broadcast: "Up, up, and away!" To perpetuate this joke, he started to wear a Superman t-shirt under his clothes. From time to time he would unbutton his shirt, flash the Superman logo and yell: "This looks like a job for Superman!" Always a crowd pleaser, creating big laughs. (Jones, p. 159)

Page 111

In 1939, the German American Bund, an organization heavily financed by Nazi Germany, conducted a rally of 20,000 Nazi supporters at Madison Square Garden. In 2017, documentarian Marshall Curry unearthed historical footage from the event, which was put together in a short film: "A Night at the Garden." https://www.theatlantic.com/video/index/542499/marshall-curry-nazi-rally-madison-square-garden-1939/

Captain America was the first major comic book hero to take a stand against Hitler. The #1 issue (cover date March 1941) went on sale on December 20, 1940, a year before the attack on Pearl Harbor. The image of Captain America punching Adolf Hitler in the face became one of the most iconic comic book covers in history.

Captain America's creators, Joe Simon and Jack Kirby, soon received hate mail, vicious calls, and death threats. When strange men started to show up in front of Timely Comics, the police was notified. One day, the woman at the switchboard received a call for Joe Simon. "There's a man on the phone says he's Mayor LaGuardia and he wants to speak to the editor of CAPTAIN AMERICA COMICS." New York's Mayor personally called to guarantee that no harm would come to Captain America's creators.

(*The Comic Book Makers*, p. 52)

The deal Martin Goodman cut with Joe Simon and Jack Kirby was unprecedented: 15% of the take and salaried positions as Timely Comics editor and art director. The success of the debut made them the stars of the industry.

(Jones, p. 200)

Page 113

Mortimer Weisinger (1915–1978) is best known for editing SUPERMAN, but he also co-created such features as Aquaman and Green Arrow. He also served as story editor for the "Adventures of Superman" TV series. Weisinger was born in upper Manhattan's Washington Heights section and raised in the Bronx as a son of Austrian Jewish parents. Weisinger was part of the early

science fiction fan scene and had hosted as a teenager early sci-fi gatherings. Together with later fellow comic book editor Julius Schwartz, Allen Glasser, and Forrest Ackerman he created the fanzine "The Time Traveler" in the early 1930s, a copy of which is believed to have inspired Jerry's own fanzine "Science Fiction." (Ricca, p. 56). As comic book editor he is widely acclaimed for introducing a variety of new concepts, but he was also infamous for micromanaging and his abusive treatment of writers and artists. Jones quotes later-longtime SUPERMAN artist Curt Swan as stating: "He'd pound on you until he found your weakness. Then he'd really go after you." (Jones, p. 284)

Pages 114-116

In *"Men of Tomorrow,"* Jones mentions that Donenfeld was friends with the infamous mobster Waxey Gordon (p. 51) and that during Prohibition he helped crime boss Frank Costello to move Canadian liquor into the American heartland, using the trucks that transported his pulp magazines as cover (p. 57). In the 1930s, Harry published several pornographic pulps and fell afoul with the "New York Citizens Committee on Civic Decency." On March 21, 1934 he got indicted for publishing obscene material because one of his publications ("Pep") had shown frontal nudity. Harry needed somebody to take the fall for him, so he picked Herbie Siegel – no relation to Jerry – a "dimwit Harry had given an editorial job as a favor to a relative." Herbie served 90 days and got a job for life. Thirty years later, DC employees would see an old guy "pouring coffee, but mostly sitting and reading the racing form." (Jones, p. 95-97)

Page 116

Julius Liebowitz was a client of Harry's, printing leaflets for the International Ladies' Garment Workers Union in the Donenfeld's plant. Julius was the one asking Harry Donenfeld to find "work for my boy Jack." (Jones p. 62)

For a history on the ILGWU see http://ilgwu.ilr.cornell.edu/history/index.html

There were others in the business who preferred to stay in the background. Harry would be the salesman, his brother Irving would stay in printing and publishing, Jack would be the accountant, and Paul Sampliner had borrowed money from his mother to be an early investor. According to Jones, Paul "was content to grow quietly rich." (Jones, p. 89)

Page 117

Sterling North, the literary editor of the Chicago Daily News, warned about comics in May 1940: "The effect of these pulp-paper nightmares is that of a violent stimulant. Their crude black and reds spoil a child's natural sense of color; their hypodermic injection of sex and murder make a child impatient with better, though quieter, stories. Unless we want a coming generation even more ferocious than the present one, parents and teachers throughout America must band together to break the 'comic' magazine." The column, titled "A National Disgrace," was picked up by newspapers across the country and inspired similar op-eds. (Jones p. 168)

Page 118

Joe Simon recalls how he and Kirby ran into Jack Schiff. The dialog is based on his memories. *(The Comic Book Makers*, p. 64)

Page 119

Captain Marvel was created by artist C. C. Beck and writer Bill Parker in 1939 and first appeared in WHIZ COMICS #2 (cover date February 1940), published by Fawcett Comics. The character was the alter ego of a boy who could transform himself by shouting the magic word "Shazam," an acronym for the six immortal elders: Solomon, Hercules, Atlas, Zeus, Achilles and Mercury. In 1941, the year Jack Liebowitz sued Fawcett, Captain Marvel became the first comic book superhero to be adapted into film. By mid-1943 CAPTAIN MARVEL would outsell SUPERMAN, and Fawcett expanded the franchise to include other "Marvels" such as Captain Marvel Jr. and Mary Marvel, family associates. In 1953, the copyright infringement suit was settled and Fawcett ceased publishing Captain Marvel-related comics. Jerry Siegel commented on the obvious inspiration Superman was for Captain Marvel as follows: "A Mongoloid idiot would have come to the same conclusion, because they both did the same things. They both had super-strength, they both wore costumes, they both had similar identities." (Tye, p. 55)

Page 120

In the 1930s, around 85,000 Jews were living in Cleveland, more than 10% of the city's population, and nearly half of them lived in the Glenville area, which was about 70% Jewish. Sarah Siegel was very active in Jewish circles, volunteered with the Jewish Consumptive Relief Society, the Orthodox Orphan Home, B'nai B'rith, the sisterhood of her synagogue and other benevolent societies. (Tye, p. 76-77) When she died on August 17, 1941, her funeral was attended by many people who knew about her dislike of her daughter-in-law. (Jones, p. 215)

Page 121

While attending the wedding of his cousin Frank in Toronto, Joe also attended a benefit at the Eaton Auditorium hosted by the Toronto Star Santa Claus Fund. The highlight of the show was an auction of an original Superman painting, the proceeds went to needy children. (Ricca, p. 201)

On July 4, 1943, the Festival of Freedom took place in Cleveland's Municipal Stadium. It was a draft ceremony full of tanks, soldiers and flags with the 28-year old Jerry Siegel as the guest of honor. (Ricca, p. 210-211)

Page 122

Joe bought a house in the Forest Hills section in New York's borough of Queens, where he lived with his parents and siblings. With his sister he often went to the Latin Quarter, a nightclub in Manhattan, where they met Milton Berle, Lucille Ball, and other celebrities. (Ricca, p. 227)

Page 123

Once a shy teenager, Joe was now more confident and went out on dates. The girls were often tall and blond. According to Tye, "Bob Kane loved double dating with Joe, if only so he could tell girls they were dating Batman and Superman." (Tye, p. 53)

Tye also describes a double date with Batman artist Jerry Robinson who tried to fix him up "with a cousin in Trenton who was brilliant, pretty, same height as Joe." They went dancing and had a terrific time. When Robinson afterwards inquired what Joe thought of Shirley, his cousin, he replied: "Oh, well, she's great. But she's too short for me." (Tye, p. 53)

Page 124

The "bris" or "brit milah" ("covenant of circumcision") is a Jewish religious male circumcision ceremony performed by a mohel ("circumciser") on the eighth day of the infant's life. The brit milah is followed by a celebratory meal (seudat mitzvah).

"The Plain Dealer" reported on the birth of Jerry's son: "A Son is Born to Superman Author. Superman is a father – at least his creator, Jerry Siegel, is. Siegel, now corporal in the army, arrived home yesterday after his wife gave birth to a nine-pound boy Thursday at Mount Sinai Hospital. Siegel is the author of the comic strip which appears daily and Sunday in the Plain Dealer. He is stationed at Fort Meade, Va., and received a furlough while on maneuvers in West Virginia. His home is at 2402 Glendon Road, University Heights." (January 29, 1944)

Michael Siegel died in 2006 estranged from his father on January 17, 2006. The Plain Dealer ran a story a few months later. The article stated that "ironically, for much of his life, he lived just a few miles from where his father and another artist, Joe Shuster, produced the first adventures of the Man of Steel. [...] Siegel was very protective of his mother, and they lived together most of their lives. In the beginning, she took care of her son, but as Bella Siegel grew older, he became the caregiver. It was only after Bella's death in 2002 that Michael started to talk about Superman, and then only a little." Like his maternal grandfather, Michael Siegel worked most of his life as a plumber.

(Michael Sangiacomo, "'Superman' creator's son lived and died in his father's shadow," June 25, 2006.)

Page 125

The original pitch for a "Superboy" character was made by Jerry in November 1938, but the idea was rejected, as well as a second proposal two years later. After the success of Batman's sidekick Robin, the Boy Wonder, it was decided to start a Superboy feature that would appeal to younger readers. Superboy appeared first in MORE FUN COMICS #101 (cover date January/February 1945) with art supplied by Joe Shuster, but without the approval of Jerry Siegel.

Page 127

In 1942, CRIME DOES NOT PAY, published by Lev Gleason Publications, became the first "true crime" comic book series and launched the crime comics genre. Edited and mainly written by Charles Biro, the series would claim at the height of its popularity a readership of six million on its covers. Stories were often introduced and commented upon by "Mr. Crime," a precursor to EC Comics's Crypt-Keeper.

The House Un-American Activities Committee (HUAC) was created in 1938 to investigate alleged disloyalty and subversive activities on the part of private citizens, public employees, and those organizations suspected of having Communist ties. In early 1946, Lev Gleason was one of sixteen publishers accused by the HUAC of distributing pro-Soviet propaganda, and like Jack Liebowitz, he had socialist ties. The HUAC was going after left-wing publishers and moviemakers, and more than half of them were Jewish. Proposing that the Post Office would deny second-class mailing rights for any foreign language paper that didn't provide full English translation was, according to Jones, a gesture against the often left-leaning Yiddish press. (Jones, p. 235)

Page 128

In September 1946, Jerry wrote to Joe: "In the past we've operated under a gentleman's agreement, with mutual trust, but in view of what has occurred since I went into the Army, and your apparent unwillingness to continue our association as it was, I'm afraid that continuing to work with you under just a gentleman's agreement, would be hazardous." (Tye, p. 117)

Page 129

In November 1946 Jerry wrote to Jack Liebowitz: "Bella went to the hospital a month earlier than expected. The boy child that was born lived only eight hours, for somehow the cord had gotten about its throat and cut off its air supply." Tye explains that "for Jerry, his son's death was like his father's: He never talked about the pain, not even in his memoir, where he chronicled his many turmoils, and he never got over the feelings of loss and anger." (Tye, p. 116)

Page 131

In an interview with Marc Tyler Nobleman (6/2/2006) Lew Sayre Schwartz actually mentioned how Siegel and Shuster approached Bob Kane and asked him to join them in the lawsuit: "I was at Bob's apartment the day they tried to get Bob to join the lawsuit. Bob's father was a very wise old Jewish guy and he said, 'Listen, let them do what they want. But you're doing good. Don't touch it.' And his father was right."
http://www.noblemania.com/2013/08/lew-sayre-schwartz-previously.html

Kane then went to Liebowitz and informed him about Siegel and Shuster's plans. He also claimed that he signed the original Batman contract when he was still a minor. It was a bluff, but afraid of facing a legal mess, Liebowitz agreed to renegotiate a contract with Kane. (Jones, p. 246)

Page 132

In the last panel, Jack is quoted word-for-word from a letter to Jerry Siegel in February 1947. (Tye, p. 116)

Page 133

Thomas Andrae and Mel Gordon republished the complete FUNNYMAN comics in 2010 and dubbed him the first "Jewish Superhero," arguing that approaching this character with humor was the most

straightforward expression of Jewishness in comics at the time.

Page 134

Although never proven, Joe Shuster always suspected that Zugsmith had betrayed them and made a deal with Liebowitz behind their backs. (Jones, p. 252)

Page 135

In 1997, Lauren Agostino, a law firm assistant, found original documents, private correspondence, legal papers and artwork presented at the lawsuit – all destined for the trash. She rescued these and understanding what she uncovered, published the material in *"Holding Kryptonite: Truth, Justice and America's First Superhero"* (2014). The book is a treasure trove for anyone interested in the lawsuit.

Page 136

The 12-chapter black-and-white film serial "The Adventures of Captain Marvel" became the first live-action adaptation of a superhero comic book. Tom Tyler starred in the title role, Frank Coghlan Jr. as his alter ego Billy Batson. The opening chapter was about half an hour long, each following episode about 15 minutes. The release date for the first chapter was March 28, 1941. By the mid-1940s, CAPTAIN MARVEL had become the most popular superhero with the highest circulation of any comic book, selling 1.4 million copies an issue. The success of the film serial inspired National's decision to bring one of its own characters onto cinema screens. But in 1943, it was not Superman, but Batman who became a live-action feature. Columbia Pictures released a 15-chapter theatrical serial with Lewis Wilson in the title role and Douglas Croft as Robin. Created at the height of World War II, it contained problematic xenophobic (anti-Japanese) slurs. After the war, the idea of creating a Superman live-action feature was revisited, also to boost declining comic book sales. The 1948 Superman serial was 15 chapters long and starred Kirk Alyn as Superman, although he was not credited in the movie where only the character name was billed. The serial was directed by Thomas Carr who later directed many early episodes of the TV show "The Adventures of Superman."

Page 137

Joe Simon recalled in great detail how people were lining up to see Jerry Siegel jump of the roof of the Grand Central Palace Building -- not Grand Central Terminal, as depicted here (dramatic license). Details are based on Simon's writings. (See *Comic Book Makers,* p. 18)

Page 138

Jolan/Joanne was coming out of a bad marriage and a failed modeling career. Reconnecting with Jerry and Joe brought her suddenly back to her adolescent hopes of fame and fortune. Bella filed for divorce on July 14, 1948, Jerry and Joanne applied for a marriage license on October 13, 1948. (Jones, p. 248; Ricca p. 227)

Page 140

Joe's father died of lung cancer in 1948. (Ricca, p. 227) In a letter to his friend Theodore "Ted" Nathan, Joe describes how dire his situation was at the time: "I have helped to support my mother and family ever since I was about 16 years old. My father died of cancer recently and I have tried very hard to work at various jobs to bring in a small income. My mother had a stroke last year and I have been helping to take care of her since she is unable to walk very much or prepare meals as she did previously. With all this financial difficulty, we are now threatened with eviction since we are always behind in the rent." (Joe Shuster Papers 1965-1979)

Page 141

The trial of Ethel and Julius Rosenberg began on March 6, 1951. Judge Irving R. Kaufman presided over the espionage prosecution of the couple accused of selling nuclear secrets to the Russians. Since the US was not at war with the Soviet Union, treason could not be charged. The Rosenbergs, as well as Morton Sobell, were defended by the father and son team of Emanuel and Alexander Bloch. The prosecution included the infamous Roy Cohn, best known for his association with Senator Joseph McCarthy. David Greenglass, a machinist at Los Alamos, where the atomic bomb was developed, was approached by his brother-in-law Julius Rosenberg about confidential instructions on making atomic weapons. Rosenberg was a member of the American Communist Party and had been fired from his government job during the Red Scare. The materials were eventually transferred to the Soviets by Harry Gold, an acquaintance of Greenglass. The USSR exploded their first atomic bomb in September 1949. The only direct evidence of the Rosenberg's involvement was Greenglass's confession. The trial lasted nearly a

month, ending on April 4 with the convictions for all defendants. The Rosenbergs were sentenced to death row on April 6. Sobell received a thirty-year sentence. Greenglass got fifteen years for his cooperation.

Jerry's letter to the FBI and John Edgar Hoover's response can be found on the website Bleeding Cool: https://www.bleedingcool.com/2013/06/10/when-jerry-siegel-wrote-to-the-fbi-about-superman-in-1951-and-j-edgar-hoover-wrote-back

The letter also lists Jerry's address in Long Island: 50 Kingsbridge Road, Great Neck. The house, built 1945, still stands.

Page 142

"The Adventures of Superman" began filming in 1951 and became the first television series to feature a superhero. It was sponsored by cereal manufacturer Kellogg's. The first episode was aired September 19, 1952. The first two seasons were filmed in black-and-white, seasons three to six in color, but originally telecast in black-and-white. There are a total of 104 episodes, the last one aired on April 28, 1958. In 1965, when the series was syndicated to local stations, Superman was shown in color.

A year after the cancelation of "Superman" the actor in the title role, George Reeves, was found dead from a gunshot wound. His death remains a polarizing topic. While the official report claims that it was suicide, some believe that it was murder. The 2006 movie "Hollywoodland" is a dramatized investigation of Reeves's death, based loosely on the actual detective of the case, Milo Speriglio.

Page 143

Craig Yoe uncovered Joe's forgotten fetish art and even showed how the characters resemble his previous creations such as Clark Kent and Lois Lane. The book was published in 2009 with the fitting title *"Secret Identity: The Fetish Art of Superman's Co-Creator Joe Shuster."*

Page 144

The Comic Book Legal Defense Fund published in 2012 a great piece on the Brooklyn Thrill Killers and Joe's "Night of Horror" on its website. http://cbldf.org/2012/10/the-incredible-true-story-of-joe-shusters-nights-of-horror

The court documents of the 1963 trial against publisher Edward Mishkin can be found online: https://www.courtlistener.com/opinion/260677/united-states-v-edward-mishkin/

Pages 145-146

Psychiatrist and author Fredric Wertham (1895-1981) was influenced in his choice of specialty by Sigmund Freud, with whom he corresponded and visited. Born in Munich, Germany as Friedrich Ignatz Wertheimer, he changed his name legally in 1927 when he became a US citizen. In 1946, Wertham opened a clinic in Harlem, providing low-cost psychiatric care for African-American teenagers. He is best-known for his book *"Seduction of the Innocent"* (1954) which sparked a Congressional inquiry into the comic book industry and led to the creation of the Comics Code. Wertham's views on mass media have largely overshadowed his broader concerns with violence. His writings about the effects of racial segregation were used as evidence in the landmark Supreme Court case Brown vs. Board of Education. In 1959, Wertham tried to sell a follow-up book to *"Seduction of the Innocent"* on the effects of television on children, but was not able to find a publisher. The last panel on this page is an ironic approach to this reality.

Page 147

Joe remembers his time as a messenger: "I was the oldest messenger boy in New York City. One day I had to deliver a message to an office located in the same building as the publishers of DC Comics. Someone from their office saw me in the hall, asked me what I was doing there, then told the publishers about it later. [Liebowitz] called me that night – very upset – and asked me to come into his office so he could help me out a little. 'How does it look,' he said, 'for the artist/creator of Superman to be running around delivering messages – you're giving us a bad name!'" (Tye, p. 186)

When researching the book, I found out that for a while Joe received a small pension from National Periodical Publications. The payments ended, when he joined Jerry in his lawsuit in the mid-1960s.

Bank Statement 1962. Columbia University: Rare Books and Manuscript Library. Joe Shuster Papers 1965-1979, MS #1709.

Page 148

In 1957, Joanne reached out to Jack Liebowitz and asked for Jerry – presumably without telling him – to be hired back. When Jerry returned to work, everything was still the same, including Herbie Siegel snoring at his desk. (Ricca, p. 243) Veteran SUPERMAN artist Curt Swan recalled Weisinger's abusive behavior and passing stories from one writer to the other, presenting them as his own ideas. (Jones, p. 290)

Pages 149-150

The tension between Liebowitz and Donenfeld was widely known, especially when the latter was planning to take National Periodical Publications public. Liebowitz was concerned that Donenfeld's mob ties could lead to an investigation by the Justice Department or the Security and Exchange Commission (SEC). Only

after the death of his wife, Donenfeld agreed to resign from the board. A year later, around the time National made its first public offering and a week before he was about to marry his long-time mistress, Donenfeld had a mysterious accident that left him incapacitated with loss of memory and speech from which he never recovered. There were rumors suggesting foul play. The contrast between the words and images on page 150 allude to this. When Harry Donenfeld died three years later, there was no announcement made at DC Comics. (Jones, p. 291-293)

Page 151

Knowing that he would be fired once he went to court again, this time Jerry planned ahead and secured employment. Stan Lee hired him for a while, and he also did some work for Archie Comics. (Jones, p. 308-310)

Even if initially hesitant, Joe joined Jerry in the lawsuit, and consequently lost the small pension he received from National. His letters to Ted Nathan are full of hope that they would receive a million dollar settlement and at the same time full of despair because he cannot even pay for his needed medication or earn any money since his eyesight is failing. In the end, his challenge of National's copyright was denied in court.

Legal Letter, Columbia Collection.

Page 152

The "Batman" TV series, staring Adam West in the title role and Burt Ward as Robin, ran on the ABC network for three seasons with a total of 120 episodes from January 12, 1966 to March 14, 1968. It was intentionally humorous, aiming at a teenage audience.

Page 153

Roy Fox Lichtenstein (1923–1997) was, along with Andy Warhol, Jasper Johns, and James Rosenquist, one of the leading figures in the pop art movement. His arguably most famous work, the 1963 "Whaam!" is an adaptation of a panel by Irv Novick from "Star Jockey," published in DC Comics's ALL-AMERICAN MEN OF WAR #89 (cover date February 1962), showing a fighter plane firing a rocket.

"IT'S A BIRD IT'S A PLANE IT'S
SUPERMAN"
THE NEW MUSICAL COMEDY

Simon, Jerry Robinson. Second row: Will Eisner, Jack Liebowitz, Mort Weisinger. Third row: Alan Light, Shel Dorf, Murray Bishoff. Fourth row: Stan Lee, Thomas Campi, Julian Voloj

Page 158-159

A thousand copies of Jerry's press release/open letter was sent out in September 1975 to every big newspaper and national media outlet, but it got a slow response. Jones describes the grassroots campaign on behalf of Siegel and Shuster in his book.

(Jones, p. 316-320)

Joe Shuster's former residence at 98-120 Queens Boulevard in Forest Hills, Queens, New York.

Page 161

In 1964, Robert Busch organized in Detroit a convention for fans of the comics medium. Sheldon "Shel" Dorf and Jerry Bails attended and consequently took over as organizers the following year and named it "Detroit Triple Fan Fair" (referring to fantasy literature, films, and comics). In 1970, Dorf moved to San Diego to take care of his aging parents and moved the convention to California. The first San Diego comic convention was held from August 1 to 3, 1970. Today, the San Diego Comic Con (formally known as Comic Con International: San Diego) is one of the largest comic book conventions in the world.

Phil Yeh is quoted from "Cobblestone, November 1975." (Ricca, p. 273)

Page 162

Neal Adams is best known for creating the definitive imagery of the late Silver Age (1955-c.1970) Batman and Green Arrow. A vocal advocate of creator-rights, he was essential in securing a pension and recognition for the Superman creators.

Page 163

Jerry Robinson's speech at the Mid-American College Art Conference at the University of Nebraska is quoted from *The Comic Book Makers*, p. 206.

Page 165

On Friday, December 19, 1975, all parties came to an agreement. Afterwards, Robinson held a party in his apartment in Jerry and Joe's honor. The party was attended by Norman Mailer, Kurt Vonnegut, and Eli Wallach, among others. (Jones, p. 320)

Page 154

The musical "It's a Bird... It's a Plane... It's Superman" opened at the Alvin Theatre on March 29, 1966. Although the production received generally positive reviews, it failed and closed after 129 performances on July 17, 1966.

Contrary to what has been previously assumed, Joe was actually invited to see the show. "A few years ago I was the guest of honor at a Special Social Event held at SARDI's – a pre-view Benefit Party for the 'SUPERMAN' Musical Show that opened on Broadway, sponsored by Ted Nathan and the Lincoln Square Academy. I was treated with greatest admiration and respect by all the guests and spent over an hour drawing pictures of SUPERMAN and signing autographs." (Letter, Columbia Collection)

Page 155

Shuster describes his dire situation: "I had a heart-attack early this year and have been under doctor's care for many months – I recently had another heart-attack and have been confined to my home – unable to work. [...] Since my recent heart-attack I can no longer drive a car or ride on the subway with any degree of safety. I constantly suffer from dizzy spills, blurred visions and heart palpitation."

(Letter dated May 3, 1970, Columbia Collection)

Page 157

Top row shows (left to right) Jack Kirby, Joe